HOW TO OVERCOME ANXIETY & INSECURITIES IN RELATIONSHIPS (2 IN 1)

IMPROVE YOUR COMMUNICATION SKILLS, CONTROL JEALOUSY & CONQUER NEGATIVE THINKING & BEHAVIOR PATTERNS

FAYE PALMER

DEVON HOUSE
PRESS

CONTENTS

INTRODUCTION

Money, a big house, a good job... Are these the "things" that make our life good? Ask many people and you will find that this might well be what they *believe.* But then, even if you just dig a bit deeper, you will find that most people know what sociologists and psychologists have been saying for ages: *your quality of life depends primarily on your relationships!*

Think about it. You can have money, a big house, and even a super job... But if you don't have anyone to share your life with... The consequence is obvious: they become worthless. On the other hand, with good relationships, even a less affluent life, a smaller house, and a humbler job can become pleasant.

I personally look back at the many jobs I have had (from working in a factory to pay for my studies to academic positions) and, you know what? The ones I remember with most fondness are not necessarily the well-paid ones. No! Do the same... Think about your past jobs... Or even schools... What do you remember most vividly about them? Your school mates and your work colleagues! And my favorite jobs in the past are those where relationships were good.

But here is a question for you. How many relationships (of all kinds) have you had in your life? Don't tell me; I am not a nosey person... I just wish you to think about them. And how many have you "saved till now"? Very few, I'd expect. And you are no exception.

There is a number being bandied about (also in Hellen Chen's *Love Seminar*) saying that 85% of "dates" ends up in failure. I can't confirm that it is true (we'll get to why later...), but for sure many, if not most, of our relationships fails.

And there is more... *Even successful relationships are not without stress, anxiety, and problems.* In fact, we can quite safely say that the percentage of relationships that have never had a problem must be very close to 0.000 something percent...

And now let's think about our lives. *How impactful are relationship problems in our lives?* Again, we don't need to go far to state that a *good part of our day is spent thinking (or worrying) about our social and personal relationships.*

There are psychological and sociological studies that show how *social relationships impact:*

- *Work and school performance*

- *Our response to stress and disease (even our immune system)*
- *Our mental state (including the ability to deal with dementia in our old age).*

All in all, they can affect most areas of our life. And we all know it, we have tried it on our skin. After a breakup, you just can't function. Going to work is a nightmare as is going to school. You often lose your appetite, you lose vitality, everything turns gray, cold and negative...

Oomph, what a chilling thought... So, let's push it away now... *Is there a solution to all these relationship problems?*

Suspense...

Yes! But hold on – I am not going to give you a magic wand in this book. Like with all personal and interpersonal problems, there are tried and tested solutions to problems, but they do require application, skills, and even time to work.

You will have to put in the time, but this book will teach you all the rest.

We will use *psychology, sociology* but also other fields like *linguistics* to give you two things:

- *A deep and thorough understanding of how relationships work (or fail)*
- *A toolkit of strategies and "tricks" to improve your relationships.*

I am actually excited because there is so much I want to show you in this book... Did you know that there are simple concepts that can turn sour relationships into fruitful ones? Did you know that you can actually change a relationship simply by looking at it with a different (and more experienced) eye?

Then again, how many times have you had the feeling that "this is not what s/he actually means" but you have been able to do something about it? After reading this book, you will! And those little daily "glitches" that feel like "wearing out" of your relationships... How can you stop them? You are about to see!

And so much more...

But there are *practical tips* too I can't wait to give you... You see, like all us professionals, I read sociology and psychology, and even linguistics in my academic studies... But it was only once I became a mentor for young people (some with very serious problems too) that I developed all those little strategies that I could just give as a quick solution to some problems.

Don't get me wrong. A quick solution can be temporary, but sometimes you do need it just to de-escalate a situation. Sometimes it can be as simple as the choice of words you use... And if you had seen the distress on the faces of these young people... And then the smile when they came back to the next session and said, "You know what? It did work!"

This then allowed me to move to the next step, which is to repair the deeper wounds in a relationship. It's like trying to reach the heart when we are still wearing an armor... Better start "peeling off" the problems like an onion...

There are (sometimes small and simple) changes in behavior, language, even body language, and life patterns that you can use to transform a relationship from negative to positive. Did I tell you that I studied *positive psychology* with arguably the greatest authority in the world, Dr. Ilona Boniwell? It is a huge field, but the key concept is simple, and we will use it in this book too. No, sorry – *you will use it* to change not only your relationships, but also to improve how you feel about yourself.

You see, our personal history gives us a lot of "personal insecurities"... These then reflect in our relationships... But if you want to have long term effects, we need to address these insecurities as well. Then, even at the next relationship, you will start with a better footing already...

Most of us cannot even see how *our insecurities have effects on others...* Like Sheila (the name is false for privacy reasons) ... She is one of the young people I told you about. She was basically scared of being judged for her family background... And that meant that she kept others "at a distance". She wasn't actually aware that she was doing it though...

I must say that she was very receptive when I pointed out to her that her approach was a bit aggressive to start with... Well, she did change it, and so did her life... Last time I saw her... She did look like a happy woman (she had grown up); her insecurities gone, she now showed her strength of character through an amazing appearance, very artistic and colorful. It was a bit like watching Cinderella dressed for the ball...

Ok, I can't get into the heat of it all now. But I can hardly hold myself.

This is going to be the journey of a lifetime for many people. From understanding the basics of psychology and sociology to learning how to cope with very specific situations, this book follows a complete path to improving personal but also social relationships. And all of them: love relationships, family relationships, friends, colleagues and working relationships, occasional relationships... All of them follow similar patterns, though personal relationships and romantic ones especially are the most influential in our lives.

Yes, it will take some time to learn all this. In the end this book compresses years of study and practice into a few hundred pages... But all will be presented clearly, and you will remember this book as "a good and pleasant read".

Now, count the days from this moment to the end of this book... Every day is a day away from having all the tools you need to make your relationships shine! And now count every day you can have *without all these problems, anxiety, and insecurities about your relationships...*

My question to you is this: is it worth wasting any more time? Shouldn't you start to improve your life right now? Is it really worth it to delay your life changing journey for another day? I don't think so... The sooner you read this book, the more smiles you will have in your life – to give and to receive...

And we go back to the beginning: *your quality of life...* Read this book now and your quality of life will *very soon* start improving. I promise you that you will see the first results in weeks or even days. So... shall we start?

WHAT ARE RELATIONSHIPS? UNDERSTANDING THE BASICS

A house is made of walls. A table is made of wood (plastic etc.) and it has legs and a flat surface... Easy. But when it comes to an abstract concept like "love" or "happiness" or – related – "relationships" it becomes harder to pinpoint the meaning.

This is not because the meaning is imprecise, or the definitions lacking. It's because an abstract concept has some discretion in the way we apply it. Let me explain... Is romantic love, in fact "love"? Surely yes. But "love of Nature" for example, may mean a lot to a tree hugger (term which I don't use as derogatory – on the contrary!) and something very different to a game hunter... And how about when we say, "I love these shoes"?

Similarly, if you have a partner, for sure you have a relationship with him or her. Surely with your family members... But most of us already find it uncomfortable to use the term "relationship" with work colleagues. Yet we have relationships with objects, like our vehicles, even, as we said, our shoes (not all of us, to be fair).

So, what are we really talking about here?

What Is a Relationship?

You will be surprised to know that "relationship" can be defined in many ways, but maybe the one with most "potential" for meaning is this:

*A relationship is **the way** in which two or more people, animals, or things are connected.*

So we cannot look at relationships as "things" but as:

- Ways
- States
- Processes

Going to an extreme example (from our perspective), relationships are states: "green and red are complementary". "Good and evil are opposites". We use relationships to describe the state of things. But even if we say, "Carole and Mohammed are wife and husband," we talk about the relative states of the two people.

I know that it looks like I have gone to the other "pole" of the meaning of the word, but bear with me... hold on to this because we will come back to it. (And no, "pole and bear" were not meant to be a pun...)

But a relationship, for most of our personal lives, is mainly a *process*. It is the *way in which we interact with people (and how we feel about it) in our daily lives.*

So, if the word "relationship" is abstract, it actually describes a form of practice. With no practical "living of the relationship" the relationship does not exist. Oddly enough this is why we sooner or later disconnect from old relationships...

I don't want to bring up negative thoughts, so I will ask you to recall your oldest friend. Not the oldest one you have now... that smiling face from your early years... Surely you still have an emotional attachment to that experience – when you recall it!

But because it's been years (decades) since you last saw your friend, you are no longer in a steady relationship with him or her... *The practical side of the relationship, the "living it" has gone.*

Looking at your relationships as "processes" already gives you a different perspective, doesn't it? We need to pause on this point, because it is a life changing concept.

Relationships as States and Relationships as Processes

John and Greta got married 25 years ago today. Today, in fact, they decided to celebrate their silver wedding anniversary re-enacting their wedding, with vows and all...

And this is the text of their wedding vows:

"I Greta take thee John as my wedded husband, to have and to hold you from this day forward, for better or for worse, for rich for poor,

in sickness and in health etc." (No, "etc." is not actually in the vows)
...

These are the classical vows people take when they get married. And I put some verbs in italics: "take, have, hold" for a reason: the first expresses the starting of a state, the other two the preservation of a state.

Brenda and Joshua too are celebrating their silver anniversary and they read their vows too. But they wrote their own and they include phrases like "I will *love* you forever", "I promise to *help* you" etc... You can see from the verbs that they see their relationship more as a process, not just a state.

And we have come to the source of many relationship problems!

Looking back, many people recalling their wedding vows will also think, "It was not what I had expected it to be". But we live in a world where fairy tales and romantic comedies end with the sentence, "And they lived happily ever after". What matters is that Cinderella married the Prince Charming. That's it. The bond is formed, it is an immutable state, and the story is over.

Can you see the problem? Society fools us into believing that relationships are "states" that cannot (or should not) change. Imagine a child (especially girls, but society is structurally sexist) ... She grows up reading Cinderella, Snow White, Sleeping Beauty, the Beauty and the Beast...

You see, these stories (as do *Pride and Prejudice, Bridget Jones's Diaries* and all romantic movies) tell an *archetype* (a basic story, a basic concept, a basic version of reality): *"the process is in finding the relationship but once you establish it it will be a state, it will always be the same and never change".*

This is so true of romantic relationships for so many people. People walk into them with expectations, they imagine themselves twenty years from now – yes, with children – but with exactly *the same relationship as now!* We know it is impossible... But this is the story we are told to believe, or at least to pursue.

So, when things change, what happens?

In most cases, *people find it hard to admit that the reality is not the same as the "dream" (or myth,* should we say?) You see, it is hard to accept that a "state may change". And if our wedding is a state, when it changes, we are out of our depth, we don't know what to do about it, and, very often, *we end up in denial.*

Oddly enough this experience is more common with women. Boys are not so much exposed to the same archetype as women. Stories for boys, studies show, are full of "action", "processes" and "performative verbs". Stories for girls are full of "adjectives", "states" and "passive verbs".

You can never stress enough the influence that what we experience (read, see, hear, feel etc.) as children and adolescents has on our adult life. And this is really at the core of much psychology, as you will know. They are *not* "just children's stories" ... They shape how we see and interpret the world and, above all, what we expect from our lives...

Now to the *"empowerment"* side of it... if you stop seeing your relationship as a "fixed state" and you start seeing it as a "process" then you are *free to build it and improve it.*

Now, let's look at these two statements:

1. *A relationship is a blank canvas to paint together.*
2. *A relationship is a fixed bond that needs to be preserved at all costs.*

Now...

1. Which of these do you agree with more?
2. To what degree?
3. What do your relationships look like, a) or b)? Note, each relationship is different.
4. Which one has more potential?
5. Which one do you feel more comfortable with?
6. Can you turn a) into b) and the other way round?

Get a cup of tea, relax, mull over the questions at your time and then we'll meet again right here, ok?

...

How was your cup of tea? Let's go through these points calmly together...

To start with, question i). *Do not feel embarrassed if you chose b).* I know it is by now clear that this is not *what relationships ought to be.* But for most of us this is what relationships look like "on the ground". And for many of us, this is all relationships have ever been. We'll come to that when we look at relationships and culture...

What matters is that by now you know that a relationship should be more similar to a blank canvas than a bond. Even if you understand it purely on an "ideal" basis, that's absolutely fine and nothing more is expected of you.

ii.) You may imagine your ideal relationship as very much like a canvas or "more like a canvas but with a bond in it". You don't need to eliminate the "state" or "bond" understanding of relationships. It can coexist with the "canvas" or "journey" concept.

Problems arise when the "canvas" concept disappears completely. In *any successful relationship there needs to be flexibility, open doors, and the potential to improve – and that means changing!*

We will see in detail that *many of us are scared of change in relationships.* But this is often *the reason why relationships fail.* For the time being, we will not develop this point much further, but we'll come to it in a lot of detail very, very soon. Just hold onto the key concept for now.

iii.) You will most likely have some relationships that are more like a canvas and others more like bonds, and many degrees in between. This is to show that the two elements often coexist in many relationships.

But it is also good for you to *learn to put the relationships you have on this scale, on this line...* That will be very useful because it is *much easier to change, improve, or repair a "canvas" relationship than a "bond" relationship.*

On the whole, *friendships are more "canvas" while family relationships are more "bond".* This may not be everybody's case, but it's a very common tendency, or pattern. As to relationships with partners, well... Some are more "canvas" (especially at the beginning), some are more "bond" and very often when they turn "bond" they also start to deteriorate. The "marriage" thing is more than a comedy troupe...

This also answers point iv.) *All relationships have potential.* This potential depends on many factors (individual potential, affinity, cultural context, life events etc....). However, *it is easier to express the potential of "canvas" relationships.*

If you see your relationship as a "bond", it is already everything it is going to be. You may put things in it, like you do with a container... It will hold memories, other bonds (those with children, e.g.) and property and the family pet. But by definition it won't be easy to change the very relationship itself.

Fortunately, very, very few relationships are 100% bond (business partnerships are, but we are not primarily concerned with them here). If you are thinking about improving a relationship and it is "very much bond", my advice to you is to *start looking for canvas elements with it now, or as soon as possible.*

Those will be the elements you will use to correct, improve, change, or reshape the relationship.

You see that even if we have to "talk theory" we have moved straight into it?

Knowing which sides, aspects, elements, and patterns of a relationship you can successfully change is the first step you need to take.

The next point, v.), or "Which do you feel more comfortable with?" is actually a critical one. I fully understand if you said, "Actually, I am more comfortable with "bond" relationships." However, if this is the case, try to find it in you to *be comfortable with **some change**, with **some "canvas"**.*

There is no other solution. But I'll give you some very good news: *you will always change a relationship by degrees.* And another piece of great news: *you can change your relationship also by very small, manageable steps that make your progress easy to accept, actually seamless.*

The same applies to changes you need to bring to **your own role, attitude, habits, communication etc. within the relationship**.

This is in fact a very important rule. If you go to counseling, even couples counseling, you will never get home one day and say, "Wow, the whole of my life just changed in 50 minutes!" No, that's not how it works. Your perspective on life can change in matter of minutes; that's why we have epiphanies. But the actual daily grind… No…

Good non traumatic and permanent change happens slowly. In fact, the softer and more seamless the change is (especially in relationships), the more it sticks and the more efficient the counsellor has been.

If you are not confident with change, therefore, don't worry! You will work at your own pace, not just with this book, but with the relationship you want to change. Actually, my *absolute advice is to avoid drastic and traumatic changes at all costs.*

There are many reasons for this:

- You don't want your relationship to become a "bumpy" one.
- You have a responsibility towards your partner, or the other person/people. You risk upsetting them with sudden big changes.
- You want to have room to step back in case something does not work.
- You need to reduce the unforeseen consequences to a minimum.

So, if you are, understandably, wary of change, I hope you feel a bit reassured and more comfortable with it now.

What is more, *we often fear change because we don't feel in control of it.* We don't know what the end result will be. But this is by *no means* what we are going to do with this book. *What you will achieve is **controlled change.*** This is change that goes:

- *In the direction you want.*
- *Where you want.*
- *At the pace you want.*

And finally, we get to point vi.) – yes, you can turn a canvas into a bond and a bond into a canvas. But this point and the point before, which deal with "changing relationships" deserve more detailed discussion.

Changing Your Relationship from "Canvas" to "Bond" and Vice Versa

Philip and Adele have been married for 40 years now. When they got married they dreamed of setting up their own homestead, but then, life was not too kind on them. Lack of money, lack of opportunities and even the fact that decades ago you could not research your project on the Internet... well, all these combined mean that they now live in a flat in a big town.

In the evenings, they mostly spend time in front of the television, and they bicker over small things most of the time... They still like animals and plants but all they do is look after their three cats...

Let's look at their story (which of course is an example) – actually, at the story of their relationship. You see the canvas that never was? The homestead was a working dream, a lifestyle dream... But it was also a *relationship dream. Because it did not work out financially, their relationship's potential was never fulfilled.*

Instead, the television "stepped in" and took that "space", that "time" that was set aside for the potential of their relationship. It is now the TV (society) that is painting their relationship (gray) instead of them.

How many people like Philip and Adele do you know personally yourself? I bet loads. I bet most of your neighbors are in that situation. I bet most people past 35-40 you know now have their private time controlled by the television.

In the case of Philip and Adele, a "canvas" has turned into a "bond", made of routine actions, controlled by some media company, but still a bond, static relationship. Also note that *the television is now in control of part of their communication.* It both dictates what they talk about, prompts them, and filters their communication times.

What could they do to change this? In this particular case, you would need them to realize that they can still "paint their relationship" even outside their lifestyle dream. The "third person" or element of their relationship was Nature, so... Leaving Nature outside has left a gap, and that gap was filled by society.

In fact, *it is very easy and common to turn a "canvas" into a "bond" relationship.* This is for many reasons, or better *forces at play over our relationships:*

- *Society tends to turn all relationships into bonds through financial, social, cultural forces.* Just the fact that your life becomes a routine means that you are stuck in a pattern, and your relationship will adapt to that daily, repetitive pattern... That alone becomes a "bond" and produces a static relationship.
- *We naturally adapt to new situations, including relationships.*
- *We naturally tend to preserve what we have (so we turn our relationships into static).*

- *Sometimes it's just easier to leave things as they are, or we do not know how to change them.*

In some couples, then, the idea of "changing the relationship" in itself is embarrassing. There is a social taboo… Imagine an old couple who suddenly decides to change all their ways, rediscover their passion etc. … I am sure we privately would feel *proud of them.* But in many places, neighbors would start gossiping, the idea of "not aging gracefully" still means a lot to many people etc.…

So, people may be embarrassed, also with the partner. And even saying, "Listen, we need to change our relationship," needs some courage. Going to couples or relationship counseling is still seen as "having problems" rather than "finding solutions" by many people. Many of us, for social and cultural reasons, are *so afraid of admitting the problem that they cannot even consider finding a solution.*

But if changes from "canvas" to "bond" (*dynamic to static*) are common and driven by society, how about the other way round? *Changing a relationship from static to dynamic takes effort and conscious steps.* And this has two sides of it:

- On the one hand, *you need to work at it, invest time, energy, resources etc.*
- On the other hand, *you can control this process and lead it where you want it to go!*

You see that we have come full circle? *Changing your relationship from static to dynamic is also a way of taking control of your life.*

In fact, *relationships that are too static or too rigid often end up being a burden on one or all of the members.* People who complain about the "strict father" when they are not just adults, in most cases such relationships have impacts that keep us "going back to them" even when we are old and retired... The examples are really many...

But now you know that I'm asking for a bit of effort, let's relax for a second... Let's go back to our example of Philip and Adele... What would you do to help them?

I would say that to start with, they need to identify the reason why their relationship has fossilized. And that's because their working life didn't work out as they wanted.

This, to start with, will free them up. You see, in many cases *we feel guilty about the state of our relationship and that prevents us from improving it.* But it is no one's fault if their lifestyle dream did not come true...

Removing any sense of guilt from the partner opens the most beautiful doors in a relationship. I hope you will treasure this, and I will remind you of this.

Next, well, we need to reinsert the third element! Ok, they won't have a homestead, but their relationship's potential still needs to express itself. And it still can, but it will need an alternative route, an alternative place, an alternative project...

Maybe they can go and help at the local city farm? Ok, it's not like having your own homestead, but it has similar *opportunities for their relationship.* The TV certainly does not.

And here is another little point I would wish you to take with you. *When a shared project fails, the members of the relationship should not attach the future of their relationship to it. Instead, they should look for a plan B, an alternative project which allows their relationship's potential to flourish.*

In the end, how many times have you had a "practical project", but the "hidden agenda" was the relationship involved? We do it as children when we invite friends to play at our homes. We do it when we invite someone out to a romantic dinner (come on, you didn't actually go for the entrées...)

The problem with long term relationships is that we then end up forgetting the "hidden agenda" and it becomes hidden to ourselves. This is what happen to Philip and Adele... They now need to rediscover their own original plan, which was for themselves and their relationship, not just a working plan...

Anxiety, Insecurities, Static and Dynamic Relationships

Let's tie these concepts together. You see, I did not introduce these two concepts of relationships just because they are fundamental archetypes... No, *these perspectives are also at the roots of how you feel about your relationship.*

So far, in fact, we have used the practical, the actual "living the relationship" aspect as the starting ground of our conversation (ok, I know, I talk more than you do... But in your mind, I am sure you converse with this book...) Now, we need to *start looking at the emotional dimension of relationships.*

Do you remember when I asked you to recall your school friend? Fine, the actual relationship does not have physical realization. You don't meet, you may not even know what's happened to him or her... (assuming you did not get married in the meantime, but you get my point...) But *one aspect of the relationship lasts much longer than its daily realization: the emotional one.*

Think about a great friendship from your past and you won't materialize the person in front of your eyes, no, but *the feeling will still be present and as real as back in the days.* Maybe it is less strong, but the feeling persists.

We enter the field of philosophy when we say that *feelings have an extemporal dimension.* What do we mean? We mean that they are not tied to time. If you stub your toe, the physical pain will last for as long as it needs then disappear. But *feelings exist even in the absence of what causes them: once you have felt them, they are forever yours.*

And, of all feelings, shall we talk about love? How many types of love have you felt in your life? The Greeks had *four words for love...* *"Eros"* is passionate and romantic love; *"storge"* is the love you have for family members; *"phileo"* is brotherly love, the idea is that of "friendship love"; finally, *"agape"*, difficult to define, but similar to "disinterested love" or "unconditional love"...

This tells us one thing at a basic level: the Greeks attributed more importance to love than we do. Where languages have many words for one concept, it is because that concept is important to them (Inuits have more than 50 words for "snow" – well, of course, they are surrounded by it, their homes are made of ice and snow, they use it to drink etc....)

It is telling that in English we have one word that you can use quite generally to say a wide range of things, from, "You are my friend," to "I am passionately in love with you" ... But I wonder how many people actually feel confident in using the word "love" at the height of intimacy and passion...

Oddly enough most of us are more at ease using this word with someone who is just a bit more than an acquaintance than with our partner. Not all of us, by any means. But if you do feel embarrassed with using that word, *don't blame yourself.* It is society which teaches us that expressing feelings is "unmanly", "childish", "not appropriate", "a sign of weakness" and so forth...

Now we are on this point... **Never blame yourself or your partner(s) for the responsibilities of culture and society**. These are such powerful influences on your life that freeing yourself from them is almost impossible, especially on your own. **Society and culture are often the source of anxiety in relationships.**

So, we were saying... Even within the same type of love, you will have different "shades", or "flavors" or "tones" etc. You may love your brother and your mother equally in degree, but the exact "taste of the feeling" is different. With your past partners, if you have had more than one, you will know that *each love tastes, or feels, different.*

Having said this, however, **society and culture promote static, even "off the peg" relationship patterns.** This has a deep functional purpose. When you board a plane, for example, you already know how to behave. We meet many people every day and if we didn't have a "ready-made rule book" to go by, we would not know how to behave.

So, we have a simple "how to behave with the Vicar" set of rules but also "how to behave with the shop assistant", "how to behave with the teacher", "bus driver" ... the list goes on! You can see the practicality of all this in a society like ours...

But... The fact is that this societal "ready-made relationships" often affect or border into *our personal and private relationships.* In the past (and in many countries) the relationship between husband and wife was dictated by strict social rules. To many of us, this is quite striking, but even in the USA or Europe, our parents and grandparents took it for granted. *Entering a formal wedding meant accepting rules that society put on the couple!*

There were even laws that said what you could and could not do with your husband or wife (adultery was a crime not long ago; and it is still unacceptable to many cultural groups). **This of course puts pressure on people who enter a relationship. All the expectations that society puts on a relationship are a source of anxiety.**

And here we come to the key point: **both the static and the dynamic sides of relationships can be causes of anxiety and/or insecurity.**

This very much depends on how you relate you relate to these aspects. Yes, it means "how you relate to your relationship" … It's not a tongue twister…

- *You may feel anxious and insecure because the **balance of static and dynamic** in your relationship does not suit you.*
- *In a **very static relationship**, you will feel the burden of the expectations it carries. Many people feel they are not up to them, which is a major source of anxiety and insecurity.*
- *In a **very dynamic relationship**, you may feel that you do not have those clear guidelines (rules), those parameters and reassurances (that it will last, for example) you need. This can be a cause of anxiety and insecurity.*

So, before you jump the gun and decide idealistically, **you need to strike the right balance between static and dynamic in your relationship between you and your partner(s).** If ideally you would like a "free love" super-dynamic relationship, for example… Well, for many people that is as disappointing as the Cinderella story, in fact. It is not easy to achieve. It is idealistically fantastic, but maybe your partner is not so keen, maybe you too will suffer from a relationship that has so few steady points, if any at all…

Like with all things in life, it is not a matter of "black and white". It is a matter of delicate shades and hues of all the colors of the rainbow.

Even the canvas... It's not easy, but what you need to do is **strike a balance in your relationship keeping in mind:**

- *What you wish for.*
- *What you need.*
- *What you can achieve.*
- *What your partner wishes for.*
- *What your partner needs.*
- *What your partner can achieve.*

This is along all the lines of static/dynamic, but also open/closed, intensive/relaxed, mutually dependent/mutually independent etc.... All things we will see very soon.

Remember in a relationship, everything you do affects your partner, as researchers and psychologists Zeider, Heimberh and Iida say in 'Anxiety Disorders in Intimate Relationships: A Study of Daily Processes in Couples' appeared in the peer reviewed *Journal of Abnormal Psychology* in February 2010, there is a:

... *"cross-partner effect, such that on days when wives experienced increased anxiety, their husbands were more likely to report a reduction in positive qualities of the relationship."*

This, in a way, confirms that relationships work as processes. What you do within it has an impact on the other people involved and on the relationship itself. At the same time, it is easier to understand the cause and consequence dynamics of relationships if we look at them from this perspective and not as states.

Then of course, *changing your relationship may include changing yourself too, and in most cases, it is necessary. But now that you know that your anxieties and insecurities mostly come from the "structure" (dynamics) of the relationship itself, however, you can start putting some insecurities and anxiety aside!*

This is an important first step.

Now, don't you feel that things are starting to change already? Can you see how fast your perspective of relationships has changed? I am sure that you have seen doors open in your mind and in your life when reading this chapter. If you came to this book with the idea that "certain things cannot be changed," now for sure you see that there is a way, but it involves changing how we understand relationships.

I promised you this was the case, and now I am sure you feel much more positive and confident.

But we are at the beginning of a long journey, and next, well, let's say we need to start reading "road signs", or distinguishing different types of relationships.

2

TYPES OF RELATIONSHIPS AND ANXIETY

S heila wakes up and her partner Stephen is already out of bed, making her breakfast (back to Cinderella and fairy tales!) She wakes up their child, Tom, who needs to go to school. She then spends some time chatting on a famous social network, before she sets off to work. While Stephen does the school run, Sheila goes for a quick coffee at a local café, then she gets the train with the usual fellow travelers and has a few words with them. She finally walks into the office and greets her colleagues, but today is a very special day... She strides into her boss's office, because she has something important to tell him...

A typical day... Actually, a typical hour or two in the morning... How many relationships have you spotted in this story? Ok, I'll help you. It's seven different groups of relationships and an unspecified number of actual relationships. We do not know how many her colleagues and her fellow travelers are...

We can see how *relationships are all pervasive in most people's lives.* But there is more: **there is a wide range of types of relationships.** This is true on so many levels! In fact, we may even venture to say that "there are as many types of relationships as there are actual relationships". But this is not very practical, because we'd end up with billions (if not trillions) of groups, categories, or types. It's a bit like when people ask you, "What type of person are you?" If you answer, "Every individual is unique," – well you *are* right, but you are not being helpful, are you?

So, we need a way of putting relationships into groups. And there are many reasons for this... One, which is at the core of our book, follows this question: imagine Sheila talking to her son, Tom, then to the fellow travelers and finally to her boss. Will she use the same language?

The answer is no. It's still English, but the choice of words, the tone, the register (formal and informal) and many other things will change. In fact, we can say that **each (type of) relationship has its own language.**

We have a special way of relating to and talking to different people... Even the online chat Sheila had before going out has its language, doesn't it? The way you speak to children, to a bus driver rather than a friend, to your parents etc. is always different, sometimes in a very marked way.

Relationships and Understanding Anxiety

What is more, **each type of relationship has its anxieties and its insecurities.** Now, there is not a precise list for each type of relationship. This is not physics... But *some types of relationships are more likely to cause anxiety and insecurities in certain ways, situations and because of specific reasons.*

An example will make it clearer... Let's go back to Sheila... Her son, Tom, has some learning difficulties. What do you think will be Sheila's anxieties and insecurities? Of course, what springs to mind is that she is worried about his academic career, what he will do in the future. Maybe she hoped he would become a doctor, and that is unlikely. Also, pupils with academic problems often become naughty and so forth...

I forgot to tell you about Sheila's boss. You see, he is a big, tall, and strong man. He smokes the cigar in his office, and he treats women with disrespect. You see, there is nothing technically improper, but if you are a woman in his office, or even a "non-macho" man, you can feel a bit intimidated, or even just not at ease with him... Again, what sort of anxiety or insecurity do you think Sheila may have about her relationship with her boss?

While anxiety is always the same emotion (at different levels), it manifests itself in different ways in our lives. It can have different "objects" and "reasons", or "subjects" and "triggers". Different relationships will trigger anxiety for different reasons and about different objects and "subjects".

In Sheila and Tom's case, for example:

- The *object* of Sheila's anxiety is Tom.
- The *subject* (topic) of Sheila's anxiety is his performance at school.
- The *reason or cause* of Sheila's anxiety is the fact that Tom has educational problems.
- The *triggers* may be many: a school report, Tom coming back to school, or Tom going to school etc.

The trigger is what sparks each "bout of anxiety" which can be a small event, a memory, a physical object or situation, and it is not the same as the reason or cause. That is the deep source, the origin of this really horrible emotion, not what switches it on...

Now, do you fancy finding the object, subject, reason, or cause and trigger of Sheila's anxiety in her boss's case? If so, I'll go for a coffee and we'll meet back here in five, ok?

...

Here we are! Let's compare notes then... Our words don't need to match. What matters is the overall concept. What is more, an analysis based on a few words, on little data, is always generic and at risk of mistakes. This is only a little training exercise. In real life, you will have many more details to go by.

- The *object* of Sheila's relationship can be her career, her life at work, her own sense of safety and ease at work...
- The *subject* of Sheila's relationship is her boss's personality and behavior.

- The *reason or cause* is that her boss makes her feel uneasy or threatened.
- The triggers can be many, from entering the office, to having to speak with her boss, even just thinking about him.

What you need to take away from this is that **anxiety has a complex realization, or manifestation in real life.** Because of the **triggers**, people often feel anxiety even in the absence of the actual reason or cause.

For example, if people are anxious about exams, they can feel it even when preparing for them, or talking about them etc. But this process starts a vicious cycle... *The more anxiety is triggered in the absence of the cause, the more it roots itself in the person's personality.*

Put simply, if you are anxious about your first impression when you first meet a date, and you keep thinking about it (triggering it), the more your anxiety grows. But the answer is not "to ignore it". It is to trigger it in a controlled way, so that you can *decrease the anxiety that is triggered.*

For example, instead of looking at yourself in the mirror first thing in the morning when even Marilyn Monroe would have "bummed herself in the mirror", you can do it when you look better. This way, you do not trigger the same *level of anxiety.*

Things in small quantities are manageable. Even anxiety. But you can even tell yourself, "Hey, I look good," and, why not... eat some chocolate before it... it makes you feel good and the *serotonin* it produces actually fights anxiety on a chemical and neurological level.

We will meet serotonin again, because it is our main "natural chemical friend" to fight off anxiety... By the way mushrooms are very rich in it...

You can see that things happen with knowledge, analysis, but also with small steps, which in itself is very encouraging and offers you a sense of security... And we do have many unexpected friends around us (like chocolate and mushrooms).

On the other hand, if you associate a negative trigger to another negative factor (you don't feel good, you have headache, whatever...) you *worsen your anxiety.* Unfortunately, we tend to think about negative things when we are not well (physically, mentally or emotionally).

So, the very first thing you need to do is this: **when you feel bad (physically, emotionally, and/or mentally) force yourself to think about something positive.**

You may now say, "Yes, it is easy to say, but not that easy in practice, is it?" Ok, I see your point. But if you suffer from anxiety, there are some little tricks you can use. For example carry something that brings back *good memories* on you, like a holiday photograph, the picture of someone you love, keep your favorite uplifting song on your phone (iPod, or whatever you use) ...

Focus on positive and soothing colors when you feel the trigger coming. Green and blue especially help you counter anxiety (avoid colors like red, shocking pink and yellow, and absolutely no gray or black). Red, yellow and shocking pink are very energetic, but in a state of worry, they may heighten it instead of soothing it.

Use lavender, sandal, hawthorn etc. These have a soothing effect, and they are very good to fend off anxiety...

We will see many more. But as I promised, there are many "friends" around us to deal with anxiety.

This, in general, about anxiety and relationships... But there is more... How anxious are you on average? Some people have an average low level of anxiety in their daily lives; others have a very high one, with or without relationships involved. What we would normally define as "being (or not) an anxious person".

Remember *never to be ashamed if you have a problem, an issue or, in this case, if you are "naturally" anxious.* I put "naturally" in inverted commas because this is how people usually say it. From a psychological point of view, that is wrong, and saying it like this makes it worse. The fact is that you are not "naturally" anxious... It is society that, working especially on your early years, has made you anxious. You are "societally" anxious... Once again, it is society's fault. *Not yours!*

If you are often anxious, you are more likely to be anxious about your relationship as well. And this has many consequences:

- Your perspective on your relationship will be less objective.
- You may end up spoiling moments and chances (this happens quite frequently, and, again, it is not your fault, but you may end up being blamed for it).
- The overall quality of the relationship will suffer.
- Your partner(s) will feel the anxiety.

- Your partner(s) may become anxious as well.

The reverse will happen to you if your partner has an anxious personality... Therefore:

If any of the partners in a relationship has an anxious personality, that needs to be addressed; that level of "background" anxiety must be lowered, or the relationship will suffer.

But we still haven't seen how many types of relationships there are. And then you may have another valid question: *does the type of relationship affect anxiety and insecurities?*

Types of Relationship

What would you use to put a relationship in one or the other type? I mean, you can describe relationships in many ways... Shall we try to come up with a list? You go first...

...

You may have come up with words like "happy and unhappy", "long term and short term", "old fashioned and modern" and to be honest, even colors can be used, how about "red and green"?

The point is, which parameters, standards, or descriptors are actually useful... Talking to a friend you can describe your relationship as "A slightly spiced journey in an old world rose garden on a late summer day." Fine, but we can't really use this as a scientific standard.

Even "good and bad", "happy and unhappy" are tricky for psychologists. You see, on the one hand they are fundamental, on the other they are subjective. If you read psychological and sociological studies, you will find them as "people who *think* their relationship is good/bad/happy/unhappy." It does matter. But we need to keep in mind that maybe the partner does not even agree...

The first thing you need is to *have clear categories to identify and analyze your relationship.* Once again, these are "qualities within the relationship" and there are a huge range of levels, but they are specific, not vague. So... here we go...

Equal and unequal relationships

This is a huge point. Are the two partners equal in the relationship? You can see business and work relationships are hardly ever equal. Parent – child relationships are not equal. Some may be "more equal" others less (and in the past they were more unequal, on average, than today). But a fully equal parent – child relationship is unworkable and irresponsible.

Many of the relationships and exchanges we have every day are not equal. And this, again, is often due to the **social roles** involved in them. For example, when you board a train or bus, the conductor has a position of power over you. When a traffic warden gives you a ticket... guess? When you have a medical examination, the doctor has a position of power too.

Commercial relationships are interesting, meaning when you go shopping. There are so many different approaches... Good shoppers are those who put themselves in control, and they don't allow storekeepers to do so. But if you go to a fruit and vegetable open air market when it's near closing time, for example, you will find that you are in a position of power, and the merchants will want to sell off everything they have left over cheap.

Ok, you get the idea that there can be, and often are **power games within relationships.** But how about emotional, romantic relationships? That too varies a lot! In some cultures, the man is always "dominant" in the relationship. This is dictated by the society they live in.

Here, we go back to that point we made in the previous chapter. *Society often dictates rules on personal and even intimate relationships.* While it is actually an invasion of your own private life. Ethically it is hard to accept. But many people not only accept it; they actually expect it, encourage it, perpetrate it, and enforce it. And the couple's family (or local society) is often the strongest agent of this enforcement.

Put simply, it is often the parents and the in-laws of the couple (aunts, grandparents and even siblings) that encourage the couple to use structures, patterns, dynamics, and power relationships that society accepts. Put even more simply, these people often want the young couple to copy the same relationship structure as the old ones. And if women had less authority in their relationship, they expect their children etc. to do the same.

This is not always successful. Lots depends on the values and beliefs of the couple, and lots on the influence that parents etc. have on them, as on their determination or open-mindedness...

But here we go... **Some romantic relationships are egalitarian,** *others are not.* In Western cultures, the relationships are often "nominally egalitarian". The female partner is officially recognized as an equal to the man, even by law and *overt social rules*. But then we have *covert social dynamics* that push in the opposite direction.

Men still earn more than women; they have more career prospects; they have many social advantages over women that can end up affecting the relationship itself. Even when the male partner is super egalitarian and the most open-minded person on earth, *the very fact that the female partner earns less can be a serious cause of anxiety, insecurity, and frustration.* And vice versa, though it is less common.

The point I would like you to take home is that **there are power structures and dynamics even within romantic relationships and that these are often the cause of anxiety, insecurity and frustration.**

And these are often hard (but not impossible) to address. In some cases, the very hard ones, *the inequality is rooted in the romantic imagination itself of one of the two partners,* usually the male one. And I am not here talking about sexuality, which can be seen as a "consensual game of sublimation between the partners". Translated: it is actually part of the solution to express these fantasies in the sexual act instead of expressing it in the social relationships of the couple...

Translated... A couple that has an equal relationship during their daily life, when they work, cook, go out, watch TV etc. then "play games" during their intimate moments will usually be a happy one. The social side of their relationship is equal. On the contrary, when this inequality happens during the "social time" one of the partners will usually suffer.

What is the solution? It depends a lot, but certainly it starts with *communicating and expressing the problem, the frustration, and the anxiety with the partner*. But don't jump the gun if this is your case... Most times this ends up becoming a row that leads nowhere. But we will soon see how you can do this in the right way. It is actually a matter of *communication and language*.

Open and Closed Relationships and Inclusive and Exclusive Relationships

You will have heard of "open relationships" meaning that two (or more) romantic partners do not see "adultery" or relationships with external partners as a problem. But an open relationship does not need to be a romantic and intimate one. Friendships are usually open, or fairly open.

However, you will see that adolescents (most commonly girls) experiment with open and closed relationships on a friendship level. The "best best friend" relationship is not actually very open, is it? And it is often a source of jealousy, frustration, anxiety, and conflict. While it is simply a friendly relationship, in fact, it becomes *exclusive and formalized, almost institutionalized...*

And in fact, it would be better to use the terms *exclusive and inclusive relationships.* And this works on a very wide range of levels when we talk about romantic relationships. It does not just mean "having other occasional or regular romantic partners".

While this is a very high level of openness, **open and closed, or inclusive and exclusive relationships have a social dimension too.** Let me tell you about two couples I know...

Patricia is now married to Robert; Maya is married to Carl. They come from the exact same circle of friends. They used to go out together etc.... You know, typical life of a group of young friends...

The problem is that since Patricia and Robert got married, they "locked themselves up" at home... They hardly ever meet other people and they have become partly isolated... they basically *do not invite other people into the social space of their relationship.* Very few dinners with friends and a glass of wine with Patricia and Robert.

On the contrary, Maya and Carl have a different approach to their shared social space. They often invite friends round but they also have an active social life... They go jogging with friends, they have "girls' nights out" and "boys' nights out" with their old friends etc....

Surely you can see that the two couples have a completely different lifestyle. There is no intrinsic problem with either. If the couple is happy like that, fine... Problems start when one of the two partners is not happy with how open or how closed their relationship is to others.

Both can be frustrating. With an inclusive relationship you may end up wishing for more intimate time with your partner. What is more, sometimes keeping a busy social life can be tiring, especially if people work, commute, have children and live in urban areas...

The opposite can be true too. If it's only "you and me" it may become tedious, boring and, what is more, frustrating. Here the frustration comes from the fact that every day may look like a copy of the previous one. You may start feeling that your life is not rewarding, even that you have failed etc....

This often becomes a problem when one of the partners works and the other does not. The one who works has a social life outside the couple, but s/he will also be tired and unwilling to meet people after work or at the weekend. The non-working partner, on the other hand, will feel bored, as their life will be isolated and lacking perspectives as well as a rewarding social dimension.

This is not unusual at all. Actually, this situation is one of the most common sources of frustration, anxiety, and insecurity, and a common cause of split ups, divorces, and relationship failures.

With a little empathetic note... The industrial world has cost the frustration and suffering of a huge number of women. Now more women go to work, but the post war society of "working husband and housewife" (rather than husband and wife) has weighed on the shoulders of millions frustrated and unhappy women...

The importance of friends and significant others in the happiness of romantic relationships is explored by Susan Sprecher and Diane Felmlee in a study entitled 'The Influence of Parents and Friends on the Quality and Stability of Romantic Relationships: A Three-Wave Longitudinal Investigation' (in *Journal of Marriage and Family*, 1992) and it says that:

"...the positive effect of network support [...] increased the stability of the relationship."

So, while one of the partners may be unwilling to meet friends and family and have a wider social life with his/her partner, this is short sighted. Relationships that "breathe" in their social dimension are, in fact, more stable than those that close onto themselves.

And this could be the starting point or even the winning argument if you wish to open up your relationship. But, once again, don't go ahead until we have talked about *how to express yourself.*

As usual, this has varying degrees too. But things can become chronic and even extreme at times... The overall pattern that sociologists have discovered is that we tend to go through phases with our **circle of friends:**

- It is fairly small as children, mainly made up of parents' friends' children at first.
- As we grow up, we widen this circle.
- During adolescence, we vastly widen the circle.
- The circle stays wide till our early adulthood (our 20s).
- As we form a stable relationship with a romantic partner, this circle starts shrinking.
- The circle will shrink after marriage and especially during most of our working life and especially after the birth of our child or children.

As you can see, all the period from roughly our 30s to our 60s and beyond, the circle of friends shrinks... At the same time, responsibilities and work-related anxiety grows… This is very unhealthy.

But then when we retire, some couples suddenly manage to widen their circle of friends, and this is usually one of the causes of a "second spring" or "Indian summer" of their relationship. Those who cannot do this, on the other hand, usually face dissatisfaction and frustration.

What do we learn from all this? Once again, *lifestyle, society, our working life etc. are often the reason why relationships close up onto themselves and shrink their social circle.*

But at the same time, we learn that *romantic relationships that manage to counter this shrinking are usually more stable and more rewarding.*

Keep the door open to your friends!

We will come back into "open relationships" in the common sense; these are, be aware, quite hard to manage but not impossible and often they can be rewarding. However, you will need to learn some important points about how you can have a successful one. This, of course, requires a whole detailed section.

One-Way and Two-Way Relationships

How much do you get out of your relationship? How much does your partner get? Again, no need to answer me… But this is a chat you may want to have some time first with yourself and then with your partner(s).

In a healthy relationship, there needs to be mutual satisfaction.

This can be a problem with inequality, but not necessarily. It can just be that one partner gets more satisfaction than the other. The reasons and the dynamics can be quite varied for this. Paying attention that your partner is happy too with your relationship is fundamental to its success.

The relationship itself should be the source of satisfaction for all partners or members. This applies to romantic relationships but also family ones, friendships, and even work relationships.

When a relationship is mutually satisfactory, there is a virtuous cycle of satisfaction that goes around the partners. Or, if you want, it *goes back and forth, making this a two-way relationship.*

But this back and forth is not just for happiness and satisfaction; it applies to:

- Satisfaction
- Problems
- Projects
- Ideas
- Responsibility

On the other hand, if this does not happen or it stops, *one of the partners becomes a receiver and the other a taker: this forms a one-way relationship.* And this applies to the same elements: satisfaction, problems, projects, ideas, and responsibility. Maybe only one of them, maybe more, and maybe all.

But it can also happen that one element goes one way, and another goes the other way. For example, one partner may be getting most of the satisfaction while the other gets most of the problems…

You can look at these as "ingredients" of your relationship. What you want to have is a "balanced meal to share equally" – or as equally as possible in any case. Every day the meal will be different, of course, but you should always try to have a balanced diet over any period of time.

Even here, ***part of the solution is communication.*** But if you feel your relationship is "going a bit one way" there is something you can start doing now, even before we look at how to talk about these issues.

For sure, if you suspect your partner is not "receiving his or her due", you can start changing things to make him or her happy. But "due" also means responsibilities etc.… It also happens that when a relationship goes one way in one element, it happens that it goes the other way for another element.

For the time being, check if this is the case. Check which elements go one way, which go the other way, and which go both ways… Ok, take some time over this.

...

Now, well done! What do you suggest doing? Maybe you thought this is a "bargaining situation" … You know what? You are not far off the mark! Indeed, what you can do, at least this is one of your "bargaining tools" is to propose to change things round so that the distribution and direction of elements becomes even and two directional.

But for the time being, just mull over it. You have part of the solution in your hands but to implement it, you will need the communication skills we are going to start learning soon.

Intensive and Light Relationships

How often do you meet with your partner? How long do you spend with him or her? How often are you alone? Do you also work together? Let's look at two extremes...

Aida and Frank wake up in the morning; they are a newly wed couple who have decided to get away from it all and now they live alone in the middle of nowhere. They don't have "proper jobs"; they work on a farm they have bought, so, after breakfast, they start working together. They spend the day together and then, at night, they seldom go out... They spend their evenings together playing board games as they do not watch TV. Ah, by the way, they have no children.

That is an *intensive relationship.* By "intensity" here we do not mean the depth or passion of feelings... No, we are being technical. We mean that *the people in the relationship are in close, frequent and repeated contact.*

Did you know that Aida has a sister, and her name is Celia...? She too has a partner. Her name is Matilda. But Aida has decoded to work as a volunteer helping orphans in a very poor village in Africa, while Matilda is a teacher in Ottawa. They think about each other a lot, but they can only text each other every now and then, because there is no line where Aida works, and she needs to go to the nearest town even to send a message. They do meet, but that is only once every few months, and for a week or so...

Ok, that is a *light (or mild) relationship.* By this, again, we mean that they may love each other more than anybody in the world, but their actual time together is limited. In this case, they are having a distant relationship.

In between, you can have different levels and stages: you may live near each other or further away. You may live together and have different jobs. Even the size of your home can be a factor in this.

And now I'm asking you to use your analytical skills. Look at the lives of Aida and Frank on one hand and Celia and Matilda on the other. Which do you think could be the sources of anxiety, problems, insecurities, and frustration in the two cases?

Take your time and I'll be waiting for you – here. I'm not going anywhere...

...

I told you that I'd be waiting... Here I am! Do you want to go first? Did you find lots of problematic areas? Potential for anxiety? I bet you did, in both cases.

Maybe you too thought that Aida and Frank risk getting on each other's nerves? Then I would agree. Such an intensive relationship needs exquisite affinity and fine tuning of personalities. But even so, over the years, this very closeness all the time may end up damaging their relationship.

And how about Celia and Matilda? We all know that these relationships are very hard indeed. The more people are independent, the more they are likely to succeed. But then of course some little jealous thoughts are more than likely to creep in. You see, when one partner feels the need for intimacy, say Celia, then she would start thinking that Matilda too feels the same. And as Celia may find it hard to resist, so she may suspect that Matilda has the same problem... and we know where we are heading with this.

Then again, when long distance relationships are also long in time one or both of the partners may actually change, in terms of personality, attitudes, values, but also physically over time. Coming back after a long time and finding a changed person... You know what that may entail...

In both an intensive and a very mild relationship, communication is essential. And here by "communication" we must include nonverbal communication too. If you talk too much in an intensive relationship you can cause a negative reaction. While texting or writing letters is not the same as face-to-face communication. Then again, if Celia comes back and Matilda has changed the way she dresses, her hair color etc., Celia may become very insecure about their relationship...

However, *relationships that are extreme at both ends often need changing in order to survive.* Long distance relationships work well only in Victorian romantic novels. I mean, they work with family members, less with friends, but romantic relationships of this kind have a time limit.

When they are too close, there are many factors at play...

Some young couples think that because they are so passionate about each other they can live together all the time. And sometimes it does work. There is no actual "rule" that says this is not possible. This, however, works better in the countryside. Why? Because they have more open spaces, and because Nature is actually a "friend", a "significant other" that you can relate to, thus making the relationship less intense and even more open. You can even invite her to dinner, though normally she *is* the dinner...

Anyway, yes, sometimes it may work. But in many cases, there are problems. Passion may be a good start, but it is no guarantee that a very intensive relationship will work. You need that *mutual respect* which you find in old, tried, and tested relationships. That sort of relationship grandparents have. People who know each other perfectly and above all, respect each other perfectly.

More than passion, you may need wisdom to succeed in a very intensive relationship.

A World of Relationships

Then again, you can distinguish relationships according to the people (animals) involved. You can have friendly relationships rather than passionate relationships even within a love relationship... And we will see them in a separate chapter. But first I want to give you the basics of how to use *language* to address problems, anxiety, insecurity etc. in your relationship.

And I want to do it right now!

3

THE LANGUAGE OF HEALING AND RELATIONSHIPS

I know that you are eager to get going, so, even before we look at all the many facets of relationships, I would like to give you some tools to start working on yours. As I said, before you put your foot in it, or you put your foot wrong, you should learn how to talk about your anxieties, problems, insecurities, and frustration. ***Using the wrong language can have the opposite effect of what you desired***.

This point is so important that I need to stress it. How many couples do you know where both partners keep saying the same thing and nothing changes? Especially in long and mature relationships this is very common. Tom keeps telling Sandra not to interrupt people and all he obtains is that Sandra keeps interrupting. Sandra is always telling Tom not to moan all the time and all she gets is that he moans even more.

This is an example that I am super sure everybody finds familiar. And you don't want to end up like that, do you? But isn't it weird that looking at these relationships from the outside it would seem that the very fact that one partner says, "Don't do this," makes the other actually do it? And in a way, this is true...

The fact is that no one wants to accept their own flaws. And hearing their partner bring them up is *seen as a challenge*, an insult, an excuse to bicker, a put down... And instead of becoming a solution, *stating the problem becomes the trigger to "misbehave"* like naughty kids who do the opposite of what the teacher asks...

So, this, however, is a process that starts early on and it takes years or even decades to become so ingrained in the relationship that in many cases you would need a professional to help. In some cases, these attitudes can become even aggressive, and what is a chronic problem can become both acute and pathological.

I have seen a case of an old woman who attacks her husband with such vehemence over the smallest matters and with such sudden impetus that it's actually shocking to witness. And this is a long story, but this woman is attacking the husband on minor matters because the husband for decades has been trying to show that he is right on other points... She feels treated as inferior for those points and finds any excuse to "score a point" and prove to herself and her husband that she is not stupid.

And do you know what he does in return? He tells her that she is wrong and the whole downward spiral starts over again... This is a pathological case I have had to deal with recently.

But it is good to show two things:

- *The frustration, anxiety, insecurity or problem was not presented, expressed correctly the first time.* So, it was received as a challenge, not as a solution. And this has triggered a chain of counter challenges that can literally go on for decades in a relationship.
- *These chains need to be broken. And sometimes, the best form of communication is silence...* Here, the husband should stop trying to establish who is right and just let her score some points.

Silence

We need to understand the importance of silence in a relationship. The example you have just seen is extreme. But using silence correctly can make a huge difference to the communication within your relationship.

How many people talk over their partner when s/he is trying to express him/herself?

Especially when we disagree, we tend to talk over each other. This is often because we are eager to bring forth our point, which "we know will debunk their point". Yes, but it does not... because then our partner brings out another point (even on a slightly or not so slightly different topic) so *we end up jumping from point to point never agreeing on any of them.*

And while we leave the discussion convinced that we are right, we also leave *frustrated because we have not reached a clear, well stated agreement on anything* at all.

It is **better to deal with one point at a time, and give each other time to express it fully. And this means being silent when our partner (friend etc.) is speaking.**

Good teachers listen to students, good parents listen to children, good doctors listen to patients and good politicians – don't exist! Joking, of course, or am I? You get the point... **Good partners listen to one another respectfully.**

Now, put yourself in your partner's shoes...S/he is trying to get you to see something, to understand him or her... And if you at least *listen respectfully, you show that you care!* Maybe then you don't understand, but what do you think is better? A partner who cares but does not understand or one who does not care? It does not matter if the partner who does not care then understands or not, does it? In most cases it will also be "not", but even if it is "yes" you failed at the *most basic level as a partner... the empathetic, emotional level.*

Now, especially if someone is *trying to express feelings, do listen with care and avoid interrupting.* Imagine it is like you are trying to get a wave out of your chest... If someone interrupts and sends it back, what do you get? A bigger wave inside of you. And big waves are not manageable. This is how **many discussions escalate into rows**.

Of course, this does not mean that you can't say a word. Asking for further details and clarifications, showing empathy, or the simple "mm" to show that you are listening are fine.

Now, do you remember Aida, Frank and their intense relationship on a farm? Some people are very talkative by nature (I am!) This is fine, but if you are, do try to get some silent spells. Being talkative, you see is great at social gatherings, with strangers, acquaintances, even in the workplace and certainly if you are a salesperson or even a stand-up comedian...

But try to understand that when you are in an intensive situation, hearing the same voice all the time in itself becomes tedious and even annoying. And you don't want to have your voice associated with "being annoying". You see, once we make a link between two things ("voice" and "annoying") it is sometimes hard to get rid of it... especially if the link gets remembered frequently...

Keep in mind that **being capable of being silent together is a sign of a comfortable relationship.** You do know that sometimes people "talk to break the silence" and this is because *silence is embarrassing among strangers...* among strangers! Not partners...

So, there are times to talk and there are times to be quiet... be wise.

The Quality of the Conversation

Small talk is fine when you are with acquaintances, and it is also part of our daily life with our partners. However, it should not be *all or most of the conversation we have with our partners.* It is sad, sometimes, when people argue and then they start again with small talk to avoid the topic and pretend nothing has happened. But at the same time, they know that it's a "show" they are both putting on.

This is by all means sometimes necessary; *if people are not ready to face a topic, never force it on them.*

Having said this, however, try to **keep the quality of the conversation high within your relationship.** This has many effects including:

- It makes the relationship more rewarding and meaningful.
- It can be a bonding element.
- It makes addressing serious problems within the relationship easier.

On this last point, imagine that you and your partner only/mostly talk about small irrelevant things like which brand of canned beans you should buy... It looks extreme but there actually are quite a few relationships like that... Now, how comfortable would you feel if/when you have to address a serious problem within your relationship? Very little or not at all.

Keeping the quality of conversation high within the relationship is practice for when you have to tackle relationship problems.

How can you keep it high? Here are a few tips:

- Talk about your hobbies and interests in detail.

- Don't just watch the news! Discuss current affairs, politics etc.
- Talk about what you read.
- Discuss work in detail. Explain what it is like and what you do in detail. It's amazing to find out how many people have only a vague idea of what their partners actually do at work!
- Invite friends with intelligent conversation to dinner.
- Do not be afraid to express your feelings.

And on this point, we need to take a long pause, a long breath and...

Expressing Feelings and Emotions

Welcome to the center of it all. The heart of relationships. The healing room of all relationship problems – the heart indeed!

There are many other things you will need, but ***nothing is more important in a relationship than being able to express feelings and emotions or states of mind.*** That is the all-important factor in any relationship.

And, unfortunately, most of us are very badly equipped for it. I mean, nowadays the "man in touch with his feminine side" is more accepted, for example, and many women nowadays actually find these men very attractive indeed... But wind back a few decades and all men were expected to be masculine, macho, and – above all – never to express feelings...

Thankfully things have changed, and this bodes well for relationships. Nevertheless, we are still poorly equipped. If some men have learned to respect their emotions, we come from school systems, value systems, work environments, social setting etc. that don't value feelings and make it hard for us to express them.

Once again, it is society that causes most of our problems. And then, when new relationships form, there are many factors and variables at play. *If you don't start expressing your feelings freely early on in the relationship it becomes harder, more embarrassing to do it later on.*

This is also because *we get used to habitual things,* and if in the relationship there is little emotive talk, we feel uneasy about changing this aspect of the relationship. Actually, *we may even feel anxious about it.*

I know that many people are not confident about expressing their feelings and this can actually be a major cause of anxiety within a relationship. And now the value of listening silently becomes even more clear and explicit.

But how can you actually say those very difficult words and make sure that they are understood?

The Language of Feelings and Emotions

Remember how we said that the problem is often that there are "chains of challenges" that started long ago (like feuds) *because the point was not expressed correctly the first time?* Let me show you two examples:

Joseph keeps complaining about everything... Clarissa, his partner, has put up with his grumbling and moaning for years and now she can't take it any more... They are in front of the TV, he grumbles about some stupid ad and she turns to him, and with a brisk and sharp tone she says, "Oh, stop moaning for heaven's sake!"

How do you think that Joseph will react? What do you think is his first thought, feeling?

...

I am sure you would agree that maybe his first thought or feeling is one of surprise, upset, even disbelief? But then, the "feeling personally hurt" will set in, and... well, Clarissa would be very lucky indeed if he took it well. If he goes silent, he may internalize the offense and that can cause all sorts of serious psychological problems later on. From insecurity, to self-deprecation etc.

So, what can he do? You see, Clarissa has put him in *a situation where he must defend himself.* Even if he does not know it consciously, he at least unconsciously knows that if he does not react his own emotional well-being is at stake. So, the most likely response in a situation of (even small) panic and surprise is not rational nor correct... It's to "kick the ball back". Maybe he will deny that he moans, maybe he will say he was not moaning, maybe he will say something along the lines of, "You can't say a word in this house," or maybe he will answer back with, "And you – will you stop talking to your sister when I watch TV?"

The last one is quite common. If a partner says, "You do this," the, "You too," answer is very common and instinctive. We learn it at school. The teacher goes, "George stop picking on Chan," and the "But he..." is expected and quick...

But this also makes a link between Joseph's grumbling and Clarissa's phoning her sister. This link is very emotionally charged, and it is likely to become one of those chains that go on for decades... Twenty years from now, they will still be pitching these two arguments, one against the other at every trigger...

The only worse thing Clarissa could have done is add personal insult, like, "You old fool". And the only way Joseph could have saved the day would have been to collect himself, swallow the pain, and say, "Is that really what bothers you? Can we talk about it calmly?"

But, as you know, these are very difficult words to find when you have just been hurt...

Now I will use a special machine, it is even more advanced than a time machine... This machine can shift you into a parallel dimension... Ready? Here we go! Now, in this dimension Joseph is still a moaner and a grumbler. He still watches TV and gets triggered by silly ads (I do too, don't tell me Joseph is based on me?)

But in this dimension, Clarissa had read this book, and she knows how to communicate emotions... In this dimension the ads are still the same, and the same ad comes on. And Josh grumbles...

Clarissa is really tired of this, and she decides to solve the problem... She leaves the room... She goes to collect her thoughts, and at the same time, *she allows Joseph to get past the grumbling moment.* You see, even if he just grumbles, even if it may look like something very small and superficial, the very fact that he reacts like this may mean that there is something deeper at stake in his mind.

That ad is emotionally charged for him. Maybe it presents society in a way that hurts him. Think about all the ads that show women in the kitchen... they can be emotionally charged for some people...

Ok, so, then she comes back and says, "Joseph, I need to tell you something." This way *she prepares Joseph for what she is about to say, avoiding a surprise, a shock and a gut reaction.*

And finally, when he is ready, the TV is off her "masterpiece":

"Joseph you are a lovely man but when you grumble about these things it makes me feel upset".

She could have said, "It makes me feel sad, tired, old..." whatever expresses her state of mind and heart.

But have you seen the difference? Have you noticed how *she opens her heart to Joseph actually telling him the truth and at the same time she invites him to address the problem in a constructive way?*

And she leaves the talking ground to Joseph, so that he can ask for more details.

And the conversation may go on like this:

"Oh, really, I had not noticed. How exactly do you feel about it?"

But for most couples, these are really stories from another dimension.

Let's look at all the steps in detail.

- *Do not react immediately.*
- *Collect your thoughts before you express yourself.*
- *Allow your partner to get out of the situation that triggered what you wish to criticize or address.*
- *Prepare your partner for what you are about to tell him/her.*
- *Make sure you have his/her full attention.*
- *The sentence you use must have some clear elements.*

1. *It must have a compliment or an empathetic phrase at the beginning. "I love you to bits but..."*
2. *It must point to the activity, the action, not the person ("when you do this", not "you are").*
3. *It must use a verb like "feel" to express the feeling and emotion. This way the partner understands that they are hurting you.*
4. *It must never ask for immediate action ("stop grumbling"...give him or her time to mend his or her ways).*
5. *It must then leave space for the partner to reply.*

This is the time to slow down and take stock of what we have learned. This structure is so fundamental to communication within relationships that we need to make sure we know it perfectly well.

Every step and every element of this structure is *necessary.* But you can add parts, for example a final bonding sentence. But you can only add positive statements. You cannot cut bits out. Now, put yourself in the shoes of someone who hears this... How would you feel? Despite the fact that this is put in the gentlest possible way, it does have *emotional consequences.*

For most people hearing a sentence like the one we have seen is:

- *Disarming*; when we hear feelings expressed honestly and calmly, we just try all our defense mechanisms (which are the ones that Sandra activates... and we all do when we accuse someone without presenting our pain...)
- An *epiphany* in many cases; people realize that they had done something wrong of which, most likely they were simply not aware.
- *Cathartic* in many cases; the person can feel their own feelings surging and wanting to "come out" and be expressed.

If you just obtain the first, you have opened a sound path for discussion, a way forward. If you obtain all three, you will most likely move straight into a resolutive moment. The conversation will turn emotional (in the good sense) and the solution in these cases is usually within reach in this very "session".

In other cases, it may take some time before you actually find an agreement. It really depends on the complexity of the problem, on the moment, on how your partner responds to it, and on practical issues. If for example you feel you need a holiday and your partner had not noticed it, it may take some time before you actually put your flip flops on and set off to a sunny beach…

But now you have a very important tool at your disposal, try to learn it by heart and practice it before you actually use it with your partner. And here are some suggestions for you on how to memorize it and "hone it to perfection".

- *Write down a few statements with this format.* Change the content but keep the format and write down a few to familiarize yourself with the structure.
- *Practice it in front of the mirror.* You need to make sure that the delivery is credible, not overstated nor understated, calm and that it sounds natural. Do what actors and ballet dancers do then; look at yourself in the mirror and correct the bits you don't like.
- *Try it out on "less important people".* You can use it (with less personal topics and feelings) with acquaintances, work colleagues, and even customers or clients if you want. One thing is delivering a "line" to yourself; another is delivering it in front of an audience. Start with an audience with "no consequences" so that when you have to face your partner you will feel much more confident. Do you have a dog or a cat? They are the perfect audience to try this out. Yes, even budgies and hamsters…

I cannot stress enough the importance of communicating emotions and feelings correctly. So, practice, practice and then practice again!

But now you really can start changing your relationship at a very deep level. There are so many different sides to a relationship that, of course, this is not the solution to everything. But you need to make an even playing field before you build on your relationship (and even your personality). And these misunderstandings and problems are huge obstacles on the way...

So, start getting rid of what hurts you and then you can improve what pleases you...

Phatic Language

Many of the things we say have no actual practical function. Example? The old fashioned "how do you do?" It does not mean what it says, does it? The answer is meaningless too. In the UK, even "how are you?" is becoming the same. People more and more often answer, "How are you?" without even bothering to give a proper answer...

So, what's all this about? These are **bonding expressions**; they only serve to *(re-)establish a social and emotional bond, to say, "Our relationship is fine."* And this is what we call *"phatic language".*

Do you say good morning when you wake up and see your partner? Do you say something nice before you leave home? Oddly enough, some people do, and some people don't...

There are many social variables and cultural influences on the use of phatic language, so, let's try to shine a light on this. Some people will take phatic language as "a pure formality" or even "small talk". But while it can be "part of small talk" in some cases, it is not small talk when it is used to bond.

But this means that some people also put phatic language – erroneously – in the category of "things to say at work, with strangers, when I am in suit and tie" and not with their close significant others, partners.

It so happens that in some relationships, phatic language slowly disappears or becomes less regular. Do you still say, "Thank you," and, "welcome," to your partner or do you find yourself using these words more promptly with strangers?

What do you say when you come home? Do you go straight into, "What a horrible day at the office!" or do you take the time to say, "Hello, how has your day been," first?

Things that seem unnecessary, irrelevant, and redundant can make a huge difference to the quality of the relationship. This is so important, in fact, that even social media have had to come to terms with it... People naturally started using letters to express simple bonding concepts, like :-), or ;-), the winking variant or :-D... Companies took the hint and came up with emojis...

There is, in fact, a study by Wang, Tucker and Rihll, entitled 'On Phatic Technologies for Creating and Maintaining Human Relationships' (in *Technology and Society*, vol. 33, 2011) which explores the way that social media users have felt and expressed the need to use phatic language on the web and its platforms as a way "to establish, develop and maintain social relationships."

So, if we feel the need to use phatic language with our Facebook "friends" why is it that we are scared to use it with our partners?

Now, be aware of your use of phatic language. Observe yourself for a day (on and off, of course), and then, at the end of the day, answer these questions:

1. Do you use phatic language all the time or do you omit it sometimes?
2. Who and in what situations do you use it more?
3. Do you use it regularly with your partner?

And you can come back to this after you have answered.

...

If your use of phatic language is regular, homogeneous and evenly spread during the day and with the people you meet, well done! Just make sure you keep it up. This, however, is not the case for most people. Some people use it more in the morning and less when they get tired. Others use it more with people in a position of power (your boss) and less with their peers.

Well, you know that people who use it frequently also have career advantages... But if you only use it with your boss, you may lose on the collaboration of some of your colleagues... Yes, it is sadly true that people in power usually receive more "thank you's" than our peers and colleagues...

How about with your family, friends, and partner? If you think that there is room for improvement, then make it a point to use phatic language more often. Remind yourself of it in the morning and then, in the evening, ask yourself, "Have I used it a bit more?"

Little by little, it will come back into your everyday language as if it had never left.

And now you have the basic tools to improve your communication, you can actually start getting your "hands dirty"...

So, next we can finally have a "rosy chapter" ... You guessed, we are entering the realm of romance, and we will explore all the different hues and shades that romantic relationships can have...

Ready for fifty shades of romantic relationships?

4

FIFTY SHADES OF ROMANTIC RELATIONSHIPS

And they are not fifty... In reality, with all feelings, like with colors, we can find as many shades as we can see, virtually to infinity. But there are some "large areas" that deserve some attention. We said that no romantic relationship is the same as any other romantic relationship, but there are some things that we can say for sure:

- *Romantic relationships are the most intimate of all.*
- *Romantic relationships are among the most important in our lives* (children often become more important, but not necessarily).
- *Romantic relationships tend to be among the most intense we have.*
- *Romantic relationships are very emotionally charged.*
- *Romantic relationships develop over time.*

And it is with the last point that we shall start...

How Romantic Relationships Develop

A romantic relationship is a bit like a day... Maybe you look at the same place, maybe a lovely cottage surrounded by flowers, trees and birds in the countryside. But while the cottage is the same, the sunrises in the morning and the light is bright at first, then at noon, colors become warmer, as the quality of sunlight changes. In the afternoon shadows stretch in the ground and colors become mellower, then darker, till you see a warm, sunset behind the cottage that breaks the sky...

Ok, I wanted to be poetic... But I bet you see the point. At any stage during this day, we cannot see how the scenery will change and, what is more, *we do not believe, or admit that our relationship will ever change, especially at the beginning.* When we are in the arms of passion, we don't believe that one day we may end up being two old bickering "life mates" ... But if the relationship lasts, the chances are that is the "evening" awaiting for you...

What is more, *we resist changes in our romantic relationships.* This is not always and not always consciously. We resist changes. For sure consciously, when things are going well. One of the main sources of anxiety in a relationship is the *"fear to grow apart".* The "let's take a little break to think" is a horrible thought for anybody. We never want that moment to come. So, when things go well, any change is a risk...

The problem is that sometimes, actually quite often, we are so scared of changing our relationships that, consciously and even unconsciously, *we resist changes even when they will improve our relationship.*

A typical example is when *a relationship needs to develop.* Maybe from the passionate stage, it needs to move into a more responsible stage... Moving in together, for example, or having a child. This is not an easy step to take... What will happen to all the passion? On the other hand, it may be the only solution, because the passion is burning out and the relationship has no other way of surviving unless it changes.

In some cases, the only option is "stepping down" the intimacy ladder. In the case of two married people splitting up, this is very clear. Both need to give up on the romantic and intimate relationship and move to a friendship type of relationship. If one of the partners cannot accept this, the whole relationship (in general terms) is at risk... and if you are still (very much) in love with your partner this is a very difficult step to take.

So, we need to *understand that relationships evolve and be ready to let it happen and evolve with them, but any change can be a challenge.* Some relationships may in theory stay the same forever, though I don't think we know one yet... But what we can do is look at the different **stages of a romantic relationship** and *be prepared for the many changes.*

This alone can *abate anxiety, worry, frustration, and insecurity.*

Now, note that what follows is a list of *all the possible stages, not of the necessary stages...* People have been known fall in love, get married and get divorced over 48 hours, and there's a few stages you need to skip to achieve that... So, be aware that *not all relationships go through the exact same stages.*

One thing though is that *with the different stages of romantic relationships language changes and the partners need to change too.* And we will address this point in detail soon. Some stages here are pre-relationship and others are post-relationship.

Stage 1 – Meeting (usually pre-relationship)

Of course, the first thing you need to do in most relationships is meet your partner. For most of us that is a "magic moment" which we will remember with fondness all our lives. And the way we recall it is always a clue on how we feel about our relationship. A typical comedy troupe is one of the partners cursing that moment creatively. In real life this usually never happens, if not as a shared joke...

So, look at your partner's eyes when you recall that moment and you will see that glint that reassures you that you are still very much in love with each other, even if sometimes it is hard to express it.

But did I say, "for most of us"? Yes, because it has not, and it is not always like that. Many people in arranged marriages only meet their partners *after the engagement,* and this has happened as a norm with royal families all over Europe for centuries.

Stage 2 – Infatuation (usually pre-relationship)

This is that time when the world changes... It feels so strange, doesn't it? The light is different, smells are different, food tastes different, even time seems to have changed pace. But above all, at this stage we can think only about one thing all day round – actually, one person.

But infatuation is a transitional phase: *in most cases, infatuation only lasts a few months.* But a lot depends on the individual and on the situation. Some infatuations can literally last a few days. Then, maybe practical reasons, or even a change of mind (of heart?) put it to an end.

Some people can control infatuations. Some people stop it because the person is already attached, and they can do it. Others stop this phase because the person is a colleague. Yet others stop it because they are "not ready" for a relationship. Or, in some cases, the infatuation just vanishes as fast as it had come.

In any case, *infatuation is for many people fairly easy to control and even end.* Despite being a very powerful feeling, there is not too much at stake, because this is usually something that happens before a relationship actually starts.

Usually, again, because there are the usual exceptions, like, well, even people who fall in love with their wife or husband after years of marriage... Or people who fall in love again etc.... Love is really unpredictable!

In any case, *during infatuation we find it easy to express our feelings, to ourselves, as well as significant others.* This is the time when we keep telling our friend that, "Oh, I am so in love with –"and then we sigh absentmindedly...

This is also the time when *feelings take the upper hand over reason.* True, this seems to be contradictory with the fact that some people can stop infatuation very easily. But the mind is far more complex than people think. When we are irrational, the one rational thought ("this is not the time, this is not the time") stands out very clearly, much more than when our mind is cluttered with other rational, analytical, and logical thoughts…

In any case, infatuation is a great experience.

Phase 3 – Getting to know each other (pre-/during-relationship)

To be honest you never stop getting to know someone, but here we mean "getting to know the bulk of someone's personality" the first key steps. Now, *how you do this really can shape what kind of relationship you are likely to build.*

This is also something on which people often have great preferences, even if subconscious ones. Some of us have in mind that the way they will meet and get to know their partner is, for example, casual. For these people, dating apps, agencies and sites take away all magic of meeting new people.

Other people like sudden intense "getting to know phases". Yet others like friendships to develop into romantic relationships. Then again, there are people who bar firmed from becoming romantic partners and they want this phase to be new with the infatuation.

Can I repeat it? Love is really unpredictable. But *this phase is likely to leave a footprint on the whole relationship.*

If your getting to know phase was a friendship phase, your romantic relationship is likely to have strong characteristics of friendship. We all know that partners you got to know as a child have extremely intimate but also understanding relationships. If you got to know your partner during a summer holiday, your relationship may tend towards that passionate but careless dimension that holidays give. A getting to know phase in the workplace instead may incorporate common interests, even mutual respect in the relationship.

Be aware of the importance of this phase without worrying about it. In a way, *this too is a low-risk phase.* This is the time when *you can still change your mind.* So, without causing useless anxiety, keep in mind that this phase too is very important and that you can always look back at it to gauge out the inner workings and basic structure of your relationship.

Phase 4 – Dating (start of relationship)

This is a very wonderful and romantic phase. Dating may last from one single night or day to... well, as long as you are comfortable with. Some people who love their independent life turn the dating phase into the main part of their romantic relationship. This has also been promoted by many US sitcoms, where the characters date for a whole series (or two, three series) before they actually settle down...

This is a phase when usually, *people are eager to express their emotions, but they can feel anxious or insecure about it.* It is fully understandable. *This is the time when most people say, "I love you," for the first time.* And this is a very difficult, anxiety fraught step to take.

One thing I could suggest at this stage is *never to say those three words unless you actually believe it.* Some people may say it because it opens the door to a stable relationship. But if this is the only reason, it may actually lead to massive frustration, incomprehension and insecurities.

Also, avoid saying those words too early. Well, unless there is a massive chemistry between the two of you, the chances are that you would look a bit "in a hurry" or "a bit too keen" if you say, "I love you," to someone you have only met once or twice. But on this, please use your discretion. You may have loved someone from a distance for example (and in this case, oddly enough, you will usually want to delay saying those words...)

And choose a great time to say it... Kissed by the moonlight is always better, or in front of a fantastic sunset... Make that moment special for both of you...

And if your dating partner says it first, *don't feel obliged to reciprocate unless you love him or her for real.* Saying, "I love you," out of politeness may cause more damage in the long term than you can imagine. Don't get yourself into a relationship you are not ready to start. Ok, love is not necessary for a relationship (for many people). But if your partner starts a relationship with you thinking you love him/her and you don't.... They may have higher expectations while you just want a light relationship. Or you may develop an unbalanced and unequal relationship.

Don't use dating as "a mean to an end" only. It needs to be a phase you actually enjoy. And *don't use dating to secure a stable relationship.* Even if this may be the ultimate end of a dating phase, it should come naturally and not because you have forced the events.

Also keep in mind that dating needs, especially at the beginning, to be *open ended.* Start with the idea that *things may or may not work out during this phase and it's no one's fault.* And if things don't work out for you, well, you may still have had a good time!

Don't load dating with expectations. You would be amazed to know that *your partner may (and likely will) actually "sense it".* People realize when expectations are put on them, even at subconscious level. And if they do, they will think of you as "needy" and in many cases, this in itself will prevent the success of the dating phase.

When it comes to dating, really never try to force things or your dating partner's hand; in a few words, *go with the flow!*

Phase 5 – Experimenting (beginning of the relationship)

The first phase of most relationships has an experimental character. This does not mean only in intimacy, though it does too. It also means in terms of the interpersonal and social shape of the relationship itself. Does it sound a bit abstract?

It is in this period that the *partners work out if they are sexually compatible,* but this is also the period when they *establish their roles within the relationship.* It is also the period when *the couple* (or more, we will get to this) *establishes social patterns with others.*

This has many consequences.

- At this stage, you may develop *habits that will then ossify* in the relationship. And this is very important. At this stage it is usually *more difficult to notice unpleasant traits in the partner or in the relationship.* But if you do, *try to change things now, before they become a habit, a "given", before they are taken for granted.*

At this stage, pay in particular attention to *what type of relationship* you are shaping: equal/unequal, one-way/two-way / open/closed etc. Once more at this stage you are *negotiating what type of relationship you want to build.*

I know that seeing it in terms of negotiation is not a fairy tale romance perspective. And you can (should) keep the romance at all costs. But add this dimension to your relationship. Without worrying *feel free to talk about directions you like and directions you don't like.*

If you do it now, when the relationship is still malleable, you will spare yourself a lot of headaches later on in life.

- Unless you come from the same group of friends, *this is when the two groups of friends become involved.* In some cases, one of the partners abandons his (more often her) friends and starts going out with the friends of the partners. This is very risky indeed. To start with, it requires an extra effort on behalf of a partner. *Having a new partner and new friends at the same time is hard to manage.*

What is more, in most cases, the unlucky partner will always remain "so and so's boyfriend" or "so and so's girlfriend" especially if the friends had known each other for a long time.

This, in turn, means that *if the relationship breaks up, the "partner from outside the friendship circle" will be left without a partner and friends.*

So, **never stop seeing your old friends.** Sorry if I repeat it, but I can never stress enough how important friends are for a relationship. There is a wonderful book about it, *Vite Normali,* by sociologists R. Brigati and F. Emiliani. Unfortunately, it is only in Italian, still, it describes how a healthy life needs some meaningful others, and friends are core to the dynamics of happiness and "normality".

Even if you have to see them "on the side" and not as your main social group, always keep a few close friends of yours with you. They are your best haven when things go wrong, and you will also need their perspective, opinions, and advice as your romantic story progresses.

- This is usually also the time when *first encounters with the partner's family* are made. Again, it is not a "100% rule"; you may have known them since childhood, or met them before. Still, this too is a very important moment. Why?

With the family you will meet the past, the social background, and values that have shaped your partner. Then again, it is so hard to establish a collaborative relationship with the in-laws! In most cases, these end up being "conflictual" relationships, but it does depend.

If your partner's family is open minded, you will most likely be welcome as a new member of the family. However, some families see any "addition" as a *potential challenge to their family's identity, history, and values.* This may end up causing strains *within* the relationship.

What can you do if this is the case? *Try not to antagonize your in-laws.* Establish a "sense of complicity" with the in-law of the opposite sex from yours. You may see that the partner of your own sex is the one who is most critical of you. *Don't take it personally;* your in-law is simply defending his or her identity and family role with your partner.

At the same time, however, *do not allow your in-laws or your own parents to dominate your relationship.* Now, *you can only do this if you work together with your partner.* It is the couple that needs to establish itself as an independent and autonomous social unit. Let me explain...

If you allow your patents to have undue sway with what you do with your relationship, your partner will feel entitled to do the same with his parents, your in-laws, and vice versa... You see, if you do this, you end up with *both sets of in laws* intervening in your personal relationship.

Make things clear with your partner, these forces can literally tear a relationship apart. Establish that *all suggestions from parents and in-laws must be discussed by you as a couple (or more) and that the decision must be joint.* There cannot be one of the partners working with his/her parents against the consent, will, plans, or without the full knowledge of the other partner. That is a fracture within the relationship itself.

- This is also the time when *hobbies, interests, sports, outdoor activities, and cultural activities are established within the couple.* At this stage, most people underrate how important it is *to achieve a balance with these and be as comprehensive and inclusive as possible.*

Do you like bird watching? Try to take your partner with you? Does your partner like art galleries? Go along with her or him... You will have to drop *some activities,* but try to keep as many as you can and above all, *share* as many as you can.

This sharing of common activities is like a fresh and continuous source of vitality for your relationship. And imagine your relationship becomes the one you will have for life... *Having a set of shared interests and activities works wonders for the quality of life in mature and even old relationships.*

Having said this, don't be "sticky..." *Keep at least one activity you do without your partner and expect her/him (they?) to do the same.*

"How long does this phase last," you may ask? There is no end-time, to be honest. People will and should experiment with their relationship till it lasts. What really happens is that the experimental side of it progressively decreases and the relationship becomes more fixed and less mutable.

However, in most cases this phase lasts within a year (not necessarily). The first few months are very experimental. Once you have lived a full year as a couple, things start becoming repetitive. An example that shows this well is the holiday together. That is a new situation, and a big one... You plan it together, you go together, you see each other in a new place, with freedom, new challenges etc.... What happens next year? The place may be different, but you have already gone through the experience of planning together etc.

"Can there be more than one experimental phase?" Yes, absolutely! There are events like moving in together, having a child, retiring, setting up an activity together etc. that *trigger a new experimental phase.*

In some cases, people actually choose one of these (well, usually not retiring!) also to "rejuvenate their relationship" or, as they may say to, "rekindle the spark". The reality is that, in fact, the relationship may have become dull, lifeless, and not functional and throwing it into a new experimental phase can be a solution. What these people are looking for is actually *a reason to experiment with their relationship.*

On an ethical note, I would not suggest having a child as a valid reason. It may even be irresponsible. But I have a little tip for you: *find small reasons for small experiments regularly.* Instead of waiting till the relationship as a whole becomes "tight", keep it experimental at a low level. For this, you can, for example:

- Seek new activities to do together.
- Find new interests.
- Get new friends.
- Visit new places.

Even changing restaurant or type of movies you watch can be a good idea. Start going to the theatre if you don't, or poetry readings. Find a nearby beautiful natural park to visit. Take up yoga or painting... Every experience is a small experiment and *relationships are far more likely to manage many small experiments well than a big one, especially when they are already showing signs of tension and/or weakness.*

And to show how important this phase is, many relationships break up at the end of this phase. If you pass the first few months, you have basically "passed the experiment", and if this happens, most people feel ready for a more committal phase: the responsibly phase.

Phase 6 – The responsibility phase (the relationship reaches maturity)

If the experiment goes well, usually *the partners feels the relationship is strong enough to take on new responsibilities.* The most important, of course, is having a baby (by birth or adoption). But this is not the only one. Responsibilities may include *any project you undertake as a couple, from small to big ones.*

From setting up home together, starting a business together rather than designing the patio or changing the bedroom furniture, *this phase is characterized by the relationship taking on more and more responsibilities.* But this has two sides to it:

- On the one hand, *it cements the relationship;* it also adds new dimensions and meaning to the relationship. If successful, this can be a source of great satisfaction.

- On the other hand, *this can put the relationship under strain,* especially if the projects are unsuccessful or if they are too heavy for the couple (or more).

One of the reasons why family planning is good for relationships is that couples who suddenly have the responsibility of a child may really buckle under its weight. Whether you agree or not on a moral basis with family planning, *a couple (or more) who plan when to have children is far more likely to be happy and successful than one who does not.*

Now think how difficult it can be for couples who meet, she remains pregnant during the dating phase, and they skip on all the steps a relationship *needs* to become mature. It is actually a much deeper set of problems than people understand... It means not only that they may not have financial means to grow the child up appropriately. It often means that each partner resents the other for what has happened (a very "toxic" situation). It actually means that they have not even had the chance to check if the "experiment has worked!"

On the whole, a responsible couple should aim to have children only once they have moved safely into this phase. How early or how late may depend on many factors (not last the financial one).

But now that you know that taking on new responsibilities can have a negative effect on the relationship are you sure that the first responsibility you want is a child? I am teasing you, or dropping crumbs towards a solution...

Be experimental and wise even with responsibilities.

Yes, because being experimental does not exclude being wise! The idea is to:

- *Start taking on small responsibilities.* Test how your relationship holds under them.
- *Do not take on more than one responsibility at a time,* if possible. And this is important... Couples (or more) who feel they can do everything with the "strength of their love" – well, sometimes they do succeed – but they do risk overrating the strength and stability of their relationship and may face hard times, even failure and they may actually even lose faith in their own relationship.
- If you can, *take a break between projects and responsibilities.* Ok, you set up your home. Now enjoy it! Take some time off, enjoy life before you move into the next step! Get the point? You need to rest and top up your energy levels...
- *Take responsibilities that are progressively bigger.* It's very tempting to start straight with "the big one", but is it wise? Do you want to set up a homestead? Start with a small garden...
- *Reflect.* To reflect, in education means to *pause, look back, analyze, assess, and decide what you did right and what you need to improve.* It is essential to the *learning process.* Use each experience as *an opportunity to improve and learn.* One thing though, reflection cannot be done in a hurry.

- *Be ready to stop, even give up a project.* Well, this is why you should be careful with children... You can't just give up... But if possible, don't think that if a project fails you have failed. This is a big lie society has been telling us for far too long. Projects fail for a variety of reasons. And they succeed for a variety of reasons. Society, social opportunities, and macroeconomic factors (like a recession) are *far more important factors in the success of a project* than the ability and work of the people involved. The rest is a fairy tale for children (and adults). So...

- *If you fail, don't blame yourself.* Ok, there may be things you need to improve. But sit down and look at all the possible and likely causes of the failure. You will find that what we have just said is likely the case. External factors must be counted. And above all, even if you have made mistakes, *it is fully natural and human.* Do not feel "inadequate"; learn from them and move on.

- *Keep a plan B.* Which, of course, once again you can't with a child. You can't say, "Well, let's replace the child with a gerbil." But in terms of plan B, this suggests one thing; make sure that plan B is lighter, easier, and less demanding than plan A.

This is a very important part of the relationship. ***Unless you move into a "constructive relationship" you will end up feeling dissatisfied with your relationship.*** This is why this phase needs to be managed well, wisely, slowly, and in small steps.

At the same time, ***this phase can and does change the character of*** *the relationship. From a passionate and romantic character, your relationship will become more "goal oriented" and responsible.*

This can be a major source of anxiety and frustration.

It may happen that both partners move into projects and responsibilities full-heartedly and then they look back and say, "But where has all the passion gone?" and this would be bad. But there is worse...

How about if one of the partners shifts all her or his attention to the "constrictive" side of the relationship and the other would like to focus more on the romantic and passionate side? In this case, you can see very dark clouds forming on the horizon. In fact, *every time the partners are not in step it can cause serious problems to the relationship.*

But to everything there is a solution. In this case, there are two:

- In this phase, **make honest and open communication a central part of your relationship.** You should regularly talk about your projects but also about your relationship.
- In this phase, **keep the romance and intimacy alive.** One of the reasons why you should be **taking breaks** is to keep the warmth of love, romance, and intimacy alive. It's far too easy to switch focus completely. Don't wait more than a month to tackle a loss of romance and intimacy. Yes, it can be hard, but you will have to *talk to your partner about it as soon as possible.* If you do not, you may fall into that vicious cycle where the more you wait the more it becomes

hard and the more it becomes hard the more you feel uneasy about it and you wait...

Phase 7 – The "harvest" phase

Many relationships end up becoming a "workshop" of activities and projects, and they keep like that till the very end. Others, however, introduce a *new element: the enjoyment of the relationship.*

This is more of an element than a phase, in fact. To start with, *it does not exclude new projects and responsibilities.* But as relationships progress into their late years, people tend to cut down on new responsibilities and replace them with "time together" and, when possible, with "having fun together".

When these become the predominant part of the relationship, we can talk of a "harvest phase".

You see, there is no actual law or rule that says that the productive phase should be all that there is (preserving romance) of a relationship. And when we look at old couples, we can find that those who have found a way of having fun have rekindled their relationship (and often passion, even sexual life can be better later on, especially after retirement).

This phase brings a "second spring" to relationships. Think about when you are old; maybe you just don't have the energy to keep taking on big responsibilities. In some cases, it is even irresponsible to take on responsibilities late in life. It's not a paradox... Just think about adopting a newborn at the age of 70...

And *retirement often marks the beginning of this phase*. But it does not need to be and actually it is better if *this phase is introduced in stages, with planning before retirement.*

In fact, retirement can be a real shock to people's lives. And this is particularly true to people who have not followed my advice so far:

- Those who have not kept friends
- Those who have allowed their intimacy to go cold
- Those who have not shared activities with their partner
- Those who have not shaped an equal, inclusive and two-way relationship.

For these people, retiring can end up meaning, "You are no longer useful, and you have nothing left to do in your life." And that usually results in lowered libido and the whole negative cycle starts, sometimes leading to depression.

If instead the relationship has already started seeing "the fun side of having time on your hands", even such retirements can turn into a great opportunity to enjoy life!

It also gives you a chance to *see your relationship as a value in its own right*. If you center your relationship around an external focus, like a project, bringing up a child etc., you can end up believing that that very project or activity is the reason why you have a relationship at all. This does not mean that it is bad to have an external focus. Like with all things, it is a *matter of balance*.

If for example you and your partner share a common project, say running a shop, the conversation will mostly be about it. And it can actually take away some stress from the relationship itself.

On the other hand, there are people who think they are "married because they need to bring up children" ... Well, that's reductive, isn't it? A healthy approach would be that they bring up children as a married couple who love each other independently from the fact that they have these children.

But slipping into one "mode" is fairly simple... Switching back into the "romantic" and "let's have fun together" mode is much harder indeed. This is why you should always *preserve this fun and enjoyment dimension of your relationship alive at all times.*

A happy couple (or more) will need *at least one afternoon or evening every week to enjoy themselves and have fun together.* Be careful here: *change the activity and keep the "having fun together" constant.* You know, very often people have those nights, but they become routine nights. The "Tuesday night at the neighbors'" sort of thing becomes monotonous and then, again, you will switch the focus from inside the relationship (having fun) to outside (keeping social relationships with the neighbors!)

So, to avoid this, keep a night every week (afternoon or morning) when you are free from all routine engagements and you do something pleasurable, fun, enjoyable with your partner and something that is not fixed. Call it "our wild night" if you wish...

Phase 8 – The post relationship (after the end of the relationship)

This is not a phase that needs to happen. It may happen or not. We all dream of the "happily ever after" ending, but most relationships end... And dealing with past relationships is not easy at all.

The key is to **try to close the relationship on consensual and friendly terms.** Sometimes it is hard, especially because your ex-partner won't allow it. If this is the case, you need to make sure that you do not blame yourself for it. Leave a door open for when s/he is ready to accept the new terms of your relationship and move on.

You need to be very firm and calm when you communicate to a (soon to be) ex-partner that you *want a sense of closure and you intend to stay on friendly terms.* Your best chance is to do it when you are:

- Alone (a park is far better than a busy road and even a restaurant).
- Free from other engagements (trying to sort these things out during a lunch break isn't a good idea).
- Relaxed (as far as possible) and not hurried.
- Both prepared (try not to surprise him or her if possible).

Here too, you must **express empathy and even sadness for the end of the relationship.** Sentences like, "Finally I can see the back of you," even if sometimes it is very much truthful, it is not the best way to negotiate a deal, and this very much what you want to do.

You want to make sure that *your past relationship won't become a problem for your future life,* and an angry ex-partner is not the best solution. This is a *must* for you. It is your main goal. And this is the reason why **you should never end a relationship trying to leave the ex-partner with a sense of guilt, of being "the bad one" etc.** If possible, of course.

If it is not possible, **at least draw a line; get your ex to understand that, yes, things will be hard to get over, but that you do not want any more problems.**

If it is possible, try also to **turn your relationship into a good friendship.** This too is sometimes very hard, and it is easier if your romantic relationship already has strong elements of friendship. It also requires you both to be ok with not being together anymore.

True, you are correct; very often the pain in one or both the partners (or wound, in any case) is so big and strong that this is impossible. But maybe tell him or her that you are willing to restart as friends when you both are ready.

This will give your ex (and yourself) something to look forward to, and a perspective to use in order to reshape the relationship. You can't imagine what a powerful tool this is. Our mind fantasizes a lot, and when we know that something is even remotely possible, we feel comfortable with imagining it.

And if you start imagining something, like a friendship, you *start accepting it.* And that would put your partner (and your friend) on the first step towards turning what used to be a love story into a friendship.

So, as you can see, if you manage your relationships well, and, of course, with a pinch of luck, but above all with the collaboration of your partners, the "happily ever after" ending is not just a thing of fairy tales!

Very soon we will also look at many more shades and colors and flavors that relationships can have. What we have seen is that relationships evolve and change. To have a long life, usually a relationship needs to do this. But with every change, there are new challenges, new insecurities and, often, new problems too.

But we have seen how to manage these, so that your relationship can be a happy one at any stage. Part of the success is due to lifestyle and life choices, but a lot is also a matter of communication, and this is where we are heading next.

5

"THE RELATIONSHIP TALK"

It can be one of the most embarrassing things to do… You think about it for days (even weeks). You fret about it. You worry about it. You try it out in front of the mirror… When the moment comes, though, your knees go weak and you talk about the latest reality TV show instead…

This is a far too common scenario. Mind you, some people are better at it than others, and, in fact, there are many elements involved in the "relationship talk", by which, of course we mean that very difficult chat we sometimes need to have with our partner(s) to save, change, or improve (or sometimes end) our relationship.

So, *the relationship talk itself can be a cause of insecurity, anxiety and, if it does not work, even frustration.* And this is why we need to talk about it…

What NOT to Do in a "Relationship Talk"

I have just shown you what not to do... I guess you got the joke... "This is why we need to talk about it," is not the best start of a conversation talk. It sounds like you have a bone to pick, that you are the one in control of the conversation and in many cases, it may sound like you want to put your partner on the spot.

And there is another thing you should not do: *don't assume that your partner is aware of the problem.* He or she may not be (this is fairly uncommon though), but first start gauging out if s/he is already aware of the problem. That would be the correct, polite and gentle way of going about it.

Do not make it into a trial of strength

Approach the whole process as a "negotiation" or even better as "collaboration" or as "coming together to solve a problem". If you change your perspective to this, already it will make it easier, less anxiety ridden, and more focused at the same time to talk about such an important thing as where your relationship is going.

Do not make your partner's faults and flaws the center of the talk

What's the point in telling someone that you don't appreciate their ways? Unless you have a positive goal and outcome in mind, it only comes across as a personal attack. This is a key point of positive psychology (which I have already mentioned): *if you really must point out something negative, frame it in a positive way and give a positive alternative or solution.*

Keep in mind that *the stakes are high in these talks.* And I am not just talking about your relationship... There are identity, confidence, emotional aspects at stake too... The same reasons that may worry you apply to your partner: *you are both very vulnerable during this talk.*

Think about how embarrassing it is to "lose face". In the end, if you want things to work, think that your partner will have to live with you even *after the talk*, and if s/he is badly hurt by it, your relationship may suffer.

And this is one of the main reasons of anxiety about these chats... "What will my relationship be like after the talk? Will it be the same? Will I feel the same about my partner? Will my partner feel the same about me?" These are all questions at the back of our mind when we need to face a "relationship talk."

The good news is that the answer really depends on you; if *you don't make the conversation about the flaws and faults of your partner, but the solutions, the chances are that your relationship may well improve.* Otherwise, the opposite may be true.

We'll look at how to approach it and structure it soon, don't worry, but I think you can already breathe a sigh of relief... Ok? Shift the focus from your upset to the solution, or it will only become a finger pointing exercise... And this is exactly what you are worrying about...

Don't try to have a "dominant position" during the talk

Sorry if I need to moan about society and the education system... We are taught that "to be powerful, in an advantageous position, in a negotiation means winning". We can see it on TV, it is part and parcel of Western culture etc.

To start with, this is not at all necessarily true. And then it may well work in a predatory transaction, where one wants to "snatch something from the other" (like taking over a business, winning a competition etc....) but it really does not work when you want to build something together...

And yet many of us approach it like a competition... It isn't. And if that is how you feel about it, then the issue is with you. You need to put it off until you have finally found the actual focus of the "relationship talk".

This also applies to how you talk, when you talk and where you talk... And now, let's turn the hourglass: after having seen what *not to do*, we can turn to the positive side and see *how to manage the "relationship talk"*.

How to Manage a Successful "Relationship Talk"

Now you know what to avoid, you should already have a more positive "feeling" about the "relationship talk". Now, step by step, you will see how to manage the whole talk, from when you first think about it to when you have it and then even afterwards...

Find the talk's focus: "What do you want from it?"

Martha needs to have a "relationship talk" this is her fixed idea: "I need to tell Paul how upsetting he has been recently, he goes out with his friends and he is ignoring me!" On the other side of the world, in New Zealand, Ari too has a similar problem with Laura, and he is thinking.

"I need to get Laura to come out with me a bit more, because recently, she has been going out with her friends while I had to stay at home." Who do you think is closer to succeeding?

Of course, it is Ari in New Zealand that has the right approach. And the right approach gives you the right perspective. This is why *you need to **find some time when you can put the upset aside and focus on what you want to achieve**.*

You see, I understand fully how if you are upset, if you have been hurt, it is very hard to see the positive. But you do have a friend here, time. You cannot wait too long, not certainly long enough till you give up on resolving a problem. But you need to wait long enough for you to have that "moment of lucidity".

Then you can just ***find and state the positive outcome you want from the talk.*** Done? Ok, repeat it to yourself over and over again, do it over a few days every now and then. When you feel that this is a clear focus that you can use. When you feel that if you get drawn into a "you hurt me more" kind of argument, you can recall your real focus and switch back to it... well *then you are ready to call the talk.*

Choose the time and place correctly

Think about the *best possible situation where you can have the talk.* You know by now that it should not be in a hurried and crowded place. Let's play a game... put the following options in order from worst place to best (with you and your partner in mind):

- On the commute to work
- At your place after work

- Walking home after the cinema
- During lunch break in a café
- In a park on a sunny weekend day
- At his place before you go to a friend's birthday party

The exercise is self-explanatory; you need to negotiate different factors:

- *The place,* which needs to be neutral and peaceful.
- *The time,* which needs to be open ended, and not squeezed between other engagements.
- *The personal tastes and needs of your partner and yourself;* if it is spring and your partner has hay fever, maybe the park is not the best solution...

In any case, *choose a place and time which is good for both of you;* you both need to be comfortable with it. And be *willing to negotiate this place and time.* Don't make your partner feel like s/he is under pressure or that you have "imposed the meeting" onto him/her.

If you live together, think about going out for a walk... Talking about problems in the place where they "live", in places full of memories of these problems can bring them back in a negative way. On the other hand, walking out of a place "laden with problems" is already a liberating experience.

Plan and Structure the Talk but Don't Overdo It

Some of us like to ad-lib, and that is fine to a certain extent. I mean, if you really are one of those people who can always keep a level mind, who can always find the right words etc., please if you wish trust yourself.

But for most of us, this is not the case. Especially when there is an emotional involvement, it is hard to remember all we wanted to say. So, we will need some planning. Now, do please note that *planning itself lowers anxiety and insecurities.*

We can go from the situation of Catherine who thought she would sail through it without planning, met her boyfriend by the riverbank and just went, "Er..." then silent to Matthew who, totally lacking confidence, went to the meeting with his beloved Charlotte with a whole set of notes. Unfortunately, Charlotte didn't like the idea of a "political rally kind of speech," as she put it and it all ended in failure and frustration.

Planning needs to be in general terms and flexible. You cannot predict everything that is going to happen, and you cannot predict how your partner is going to react. *Keep your plan simple enough so that you can commit it to memory very easily.*

Three to five key points and maybe a few key words are all you need, but in particular, make sure you have *your goal* clearly in mind.

Of the key words, *think carefully about how you can describe how you felt or feel*. Remember that expressing correctly how you feel as we said in Chapter 3 is the key to success. *Follow the structure in Chapter 3, "The language of feelings and emotions".*

Also *allow your partner to express his or her feelings too after you have (or vice versa).*

That should already make sure that *you both feel equal and empowered in the talk.*

Divide the talk into three parts:

- *Expressing the problem.*
- *Discussing the solution.*
- *Agreeing on the steps to take next.*

So, after you both have expressed your feelings, you can, if you feel like it, *forgive each other*. This would be ideal. If you do, do it with a smile and a hug etc. But this should not mean that everything is ok. This should be a first step to make sure things are not repeated.

Next, you can move into the second step: *negotiating the solution.*

This is a different type of talk altogether. This is the actual negotiation. Don't try to impose your solution, but *present it as practical, show its benefits and argue it.*

But you should also be ready to *adapt it, change it, and incorporate your partner's suggestions.*

And how about if your partner has another solution in mind? Be prepared for this possibility and be very *open to your partner's solution.* This is not a matter of "who wins". It is a matter of *choosing the best solution.* And if you think your partner's is better, so be it.

Make sure *you pause on the solution you have chosen; it needs to be very clear to both of you.* Close with a toast, an ice cream, a small celebration of any kind... That will highlight the positive aspect of the relationship.

You can now ***agree on what steps to take next.*** This is the "implementation" phase of the solution. But I would add a little element which I will tell you at the end...

Try to be quite *specific but relaxed with this step.* If the problem is the same as Ari and Laura's and you wanted your partner to spend more time with you, maybe you should do as follows. On the one hand, choose one specific day (two, three etc....) which you two will spend alone, together and having fun. On the other hand, you should still allow your partner to meet with his or her friends freely, as long as s/he honors her side of the deal with you.

Also decide *when to start* and, if it is a complex solution, *break up the solution into manageable steps and outline a sequence and timing for them.* This should not, however, become a source of stress. It should become a pleasurable project. Give yourself time; take it easy!

Ah, I was forgetting... The last tip... ***Take some time to bond after the talk.*** You see, making sure that your relationship is as sound and as loving as before is essential at this stage. Even you achieve a lot with the "relationship talk", it is never easy, and you have been through a tough negotiation, you have used logic and reason...

All this distracts you from the emotional and deep value and dimension of your relationship; so, this is time to "re-establish that emotional bond between the partners".

Is Rehearsing the "Relationship Talk" a Good Idea?

Like with all important things, yes. But don't turn it into a 24-episode TV series

Rehearse only bits of it, like the "expressing feelings and emotion" structure or routine. This is to make sure you don't get the wrong words out at the salient moments. Rehearse maybe some key parts and points. Find sentences or concepts you have in mind that you must make sure you say and rehearse only those.

But *only rehearse key bits and only till you feel fairly confident with them.* You *need to avoid that the "perfect delivery" ends up being a "soulless delivery".* If you rehearse too much, you will end up just "saying the words" without expressing the feelings. And that would be bad for the whole talk.

Do you know that one of the main problems with movie actors and actresses is that if they don't get the delivery right in the first few takes; the risk is that even they will fail to "express" the lines?

And have you ever tried to repeat a word over and over again till it has no meaning? This phenomenon is well known, and it is called *"semantic saturation".* On a different level, this happens to "over-rehearsed lines" too.

And *do not rehearse the whole talk; this can be very counterproductive.* To start with, you do not know how it will go. If you rehearse it and your partner leads it in another direction, you will find it harder to adapt, change and in the end get what you want.

What is more, if you rehearse it all, you may end up thinking that if it does not go as you have planned, it is not a success. And it will not go exactly as you planned. Even if it is successful! So, rehearsing the whole talk (like politicians do with speeches and actors with scripts) will end up being a source of frustration...

How to Behave During the Talk

Once you have a good idea of what you want to get from the talk, of what you are going to say (in general terms) and how the talk will be structured, you can "face the music" with much more confidence and a stronger heart.

But like with all "live events" there are always surprises and unforeseen events. What can you do then? Here are a few handy tips for you...

Be flexible

Be ready to change tack and follow your partner. This does not mean "giving up"; it means collaborating. Keep your goal in mind, but don't become too strict with the ways you can follow in order to achieve it.

Be calm

Try to be calm and in control of yourself, rather than in control of the conversation. If you become upset, do take some time off. Five minutes to cool down if necessary, or even more, must be granted to you and to your partner every time they are needed.

Which leads us to the next point...

Take breaks

If you or your partner get tired, upset, nervous, tearful, confused etc., be absolutely ready to take a break. Even if the talk goes on for too long...

You need to *focus on getting things right, with calm and serenity (as far as possible) rather than getting things "done quickly".*

And on this point...

Be ready to adjourn

What an official sounding word... But the point is that if you cannot reach an agreement, and you are feeling tired, frustrated, or in general you feel that you are not moving forward, stop the talk and agree to meet again another time.

But another time does not mean "some time"; decide the time and place and make it as soon as possible. Just give each other enough time to "collect your thoughts and reflect" and then meet again.

A long wait can be frustrating and even induce anxiety. So, "next week" is a bit too late, and if it can be done within a day or two, do it.

Keep to the point – don't start chains or "go down memory lane"

Try to stick to your points, the ones you had planned, as far as possible. Above all, avoid making long lists of "the times when you..." or "things that you..." These can be taken as "insisting on something painful". They can be felt more like an accusation than a chat with a solution in mind.

At the same time, if past memories come up, just pick the positive ones to share with your partner. If negative ones come up, avoid going "down memory lane" with them... it will have the same effect as before: *your partner will feel like s/he is on trial while you are reading the counts of accusations to him/her.*

Fend off eventual "attacks"

This is very important, and we will look into it in more detail next, when we talk about "de-escalating", a skill which is so useful in all relationships of all types and it comes in handy in so many situations...

Understand that your partner – through past experiences, maybe – could have the wrong idea of what the whole exercise is about... We are "programmed" to react to any criticism with "but you" or "how about the time when you?" etc.... We look at these situations as a "match" rather than a collaboration. And this can happen even if you use the most sympathetic, soft and welcoming words...

The best solution is to ignore any "attacks". This can be hard, and we will see how you can be successful at this next, but for now, think that if you fall into that logic of "you against me" the whole talk is going to turn into an argument.

So, *be very aware of any signs of the talk turning into an argument.* When you spot them:

- *Ignore them*
- *Defuse them (even with a joke)*
- *Do not return them*

- *If necessary, walk away and take a break*

If you can, do tell your partner that your intention was not to have an argument, and that this is not the time to bring up all the little disagreements and problems you have...

And this leads us straight into the next chapter. In fact, a very, very important one on de-escalating situations... And even the very, very best and most romantic relationships sometimes have "their moments". Better be prepared then!

6

DEALING WITH ARGUMENTS IN YOUR RELATIONSHIP

"... And they lived happily ever after" – bickering every now and then and with the occasional epic row. Let's face reality, even the most close-knit couple will have the occasional crisis. Of course, there are exceptions, but they are very rare. And we need to be prepared for all eventualities.

In fact, we all have first-hand experience of rows... And here is where we will start. It is an unpleasant thought, I know, but think about a row you remember well. Even one you have seen in a movie if you want to keep some detachment.

Just go through it like a story, just a normal narrative first. Then, try to identify this:

- The phrase or action that *triggered* the argument.
- The *response* to that trigger.

- The *escalation.*
- The *tipping point,* which is when the row actually became "full out".
- If you can, also look at before the row or argument, and see if one of the two people gave any signs of *"being closed to others"*, of not wanting to deal with any challenge, like the way s/he walked, talked, looked, sat etc.…

As usual, take your time… I actually live in a cupboard and come out only when you need me…

…

Out of the cupboard then… Take a deep breath. I fully understand the emotional price of remembering negative episodes… Anyway, have you identified the *trigger, response, escalation,* and *tipping point?*

I bet you have, and you have likely found signs of closure in one of the participants too.

And if you have, you now know…

The Stages of an Argument or Row

There is a huge difference between having a disagreement and having an argument, or a row. A disagreement is simply a matter of having different opinions; in a row, you have *a clash and signs of hostility.*

And rows or arguments have a very specific pattern. We all recognize it, at least subconsciously. In fact, we all *know* when an argument is about to burst between two people because we recognize the stages.

The pre-stage

Even before the row, there are usually elements that can bring about the clash. These may be many, like long term hostility or competition between the people involved, or one of the people having had a bad day (signaled though verbal and nonverbal signs, as we said – signs that are not picked up by the other person, most often).

Now, imagine a child at school, her name is Namina... She is really sulking and refusing to collaborate... She is looking out of the window, and she looks angry. The teacher does not know why Namina is behaving like this. But she is worried and keeps looking at her and she goes to her. She also goes over to her side of the classroom quite often, and then she tries to talk to Namina...

Of course, to no avail... Namina, instead of collaborating, gets even more upset.

Now, can you see what has gone wrong here? Look at this example and see what has happened that has spoiled the teacher's effort?

...

It's full of woodworms in my cupboard, I have just found out... Did you have time to think about it? You may have come up with a few answers like:

- They are in front of other people, so, this is not the place to talk to Namina, as she may want to keep her privacy.

- Maybe the teacher is the cause of Namina's upset and she does not know it?
- The teacher missed to read Namina' "keep off" body language.
- Maybe Namina would like a friend to talk to her?
- Going over to her side repeatedly may have worsened the situation.

All these could be good reasons. The key point is to *identify pre-crisis or pre-argument signs in others.* And by all means ***if you see an argument coming, do not trigger it, step away!***

Really the only solution at this stage is to ***allow the other person time to sort out his or her problems, to stay alone and cool down.***

The trigger

This can be very small. It can be a word, a gesture, even just a look.

The problem is that ***the trigger is not the real cause of the argument, but it often becomes the center of the argument itself.*** This means that *in arguments, people often talk and argue about the wrong point...*

You all know that when couples (especially small ones) argue about small things, in reality they are bickering about "something else". This happens so often, "Eat with your mouth closed," sometimes can mean "We never have quality time together..."

In the short run, the people concerned are trapped in a *topic that will not give any real solution to the real problem.* In serious cases, then, when there is a long history of disagreement and problems, this can become a pure "exercise in hostility". At this stage, the topic is totally irrelevant... That is a pathological stage. But it is far more common than we might imagine.

In the long term, the couple often use this "shift of focus on the trigger" to avoid facing the real problem, which is often more painful, more difficult to approach and solve...

Now, hold onto this information for a few minutes. You will need it when we talk about the solutions.

The response to the trigger

If the trigger goes unnoticed, the argument does not start (and this is a hint...) But if it is picked up with hostility, then the argument is in the making. In this case, the trigger is seen as any or all of these:

- A (personal) challenge
- An act of hostility
- Unfair
- A signal that the other person wants to argue
- A challenge of one's position

The response, then, will be one of *confrontation, rather than reconciliation.*

There are also some typical qualities of this response, like it is quick, it is negative, it is not thoughtful, it is often loud etc.

But while you can see that with a proper analysis of the dynamics of arguments (like this) you can already see possible paths to a solution, I will ask you to wait for few minutes... We will get to it soon.

The escalation

After the trigger it is usually hard to calm things down. The opposition of the two parts becomes bigger and bigger, stronger and stronger... words become louder and louder and *the more the exchange goes on the further apart the people involved become.*

This is a phase called escalation. Do you remember Namina? I didn't tell you what happened after the teacher asked her:

"What's wrong with you, Namina?" (Wrong question – trigger!)

"Nothing, Miss," answers Namina with a grunt and looking away.

"It can't be nothing," replies the teacher.

"I said nothing," insists Namina.

"You are sulking, Namina, why?" the teacher says, her voice louder.

"Why are you hassling me?" Namina's voice too gets louder.

"How dare you talk to me like that!" shouts the teacher.

Namina storms out of the classroom.

Escalation is characterized by:

- None of the participants giving up.
- Increasing intensity.

- Increasing loudness.
- Stronger and stronger words.
- Sometimes, even aggressive gestures.

Escalation pushes one of the participants to take action, in some cases, this is shouting so loud that the other is silenced. In other cases, it can actually get physical. Namina, a child, actually has the best reaction she could have: she storms out, yes, breaking school rules, but she actually stops the argument the only way she can. High five Namina! You are wiser than the teacher! And we'll see why in the solution part of this chapter.

The tipping point

The *escalation forces a tipping point: because none of the participants is willing to give up, one of them needs to take drastic action to put an end to the argument.* This is also the most dangerous point in an argument. It is usually at this stage that, if one person has aggressive tendencies, things become physical.

Even in arguments among thugs the dynamics are the same and there is little expectation of violence till the tipping point. Looking at them (even how their arguments are portrayed realistically in films) you can see all the stages leading up to what is often a physical reaction.

Then, of course, in movies there are friends who split them up or things become really nasty.

But a violent end to arguments is comparatively rare. In most cases, there is a *total breakdown of communication, accompanied by loud and angry words and a breakup of some sort.* I don't mean a breaking up of a relationship – not necessarily, though there are relationships that break up after arguments, quite a few indeed! In case one of the partners has the cool head Namina has, the breakup can just be one of the partners walking away.

Now you know how the teacher felt... She felt Namina's walking away is a challenge to her role and authority, even an insult... And when the relationship is personal and even more intimate, the walking away can be even tougher, often followed by tears etc.

But some people have this as their exist strategy, like Namina. They are people who, for whatever reason (it can be a very personal reason, like, in some cases children who often witnessed their parents arguing) cannot stand an argument. Their gut reaction is to walk away.

If your partner is one of these people, *respect his or her "strategy"*. It is actually a good and wise one. But the key thing is that *you should not take it as a personal insult or challenge or disrespect. Nor should you necessarily think your partner does not want to face the problem you have. It may just be that your partner will not face the problem during an argument.*

If you notice this attitude in your partner, try to discuss the actual problem (not the trigger) with serenity, a bit like we said in the "relationship talk" chapter. If you notice that your partner is more open to talking there, then you are onto a solution.

And talking about solutions...

How to Avoid a Bad Argument

We have already seen some solutions, and there are quite a few we are going to see right now. Before we do, however, we need to look at some general points.

You need to understand the stages of arguments to apply the right solution. And you have just seen them all... so, we are at a good point.

At each stage, you have a way out. So, don't worry if the argument has been triggered, you still have a way of getting out of it, maybe even with a smile!

Your aim to avoid the tipping point at all costs. You see, if you look at a bad argument from its "climax", from its final point, you realize that all that goes on before, while bad, is far less painful. So, whenever an argument starts, please understand that it is going to become more and more painful the longer it goes on, so, as a consequence...

...Try to stop the argument at as early a stage as possible. Put your ego and your immediate goals (that may be "getting it off your chest" or "venting your anger" or "this time I'm not letting him/her off the hook"). Instead, *focus on your long-term goal, which is to have a happy relationship with as little tension as possible and to solve problems...*

If you argue often, you will notice that at first you will manage to stop the tipping just before it happens or to "soften it" while it still happens. Then, after some time, you will usually stop the arguments at increasingly earlier stages. Habits, even arguing habits, are hard to break and progress is usually gradual... But keep at it and in the meantime focus on how more relaxed, and happier your relationship is gradually becoming.

Avoiding the Bad Argument

We have already touched on it. The best way out and the earliest way out is to *understand when your partner is "closed" and avoid nagging or teasing her or him.* The best thing the teacher should have done is what Namina was asking with her body language and attitude: leave her alone. You will be amazed at how common Namina's story is in classrooms... And how some teachers still don't get the key strategy point: if a student is angry, it may not be about you, and don't take it personally. Leave the pupil alone and if you don't, then it may become about you...

The same often applies to partners. How many times have partners quarreled because one of them was tired and the other didn't understand it? You get home from work and you are knackered. That's really not the time to have a trigger thrown your way, like, "Once more you have forgotten to put out the garbage!"

You understand how you feel when these things happen to you, right? You think, "I am exhausted, can't s/he see it?" Then, as things happen again and again, the odd thought like, "S/he's done it again," or even, "Now s/he is doing it on purpose," sneak in and make things even worse.

Then again, we can even take things personally, with thoughts along the lines of, "If s/he has not seen how exhausted I am, it means s/he has not even looked at me!" And this is quite a sad thought, really. But maybe s/he has not been able to read your nonverbal cues, like you slumping into the sofa... Maybe s/he is tired too and sees you on the sofa while s/he is cooking...

Now, I'm not taking sides (and this is the wisest thing to do when you see people arguing...), but I am trying to make you think from your partner's perspective. Surely you have been in both roles, have you not?

So, the first trick is to **understand when your partner is "closed" and that at this stage, even things that may have a very innocent intention can be seen as "triggers".**

Defuse the Trigger

"But how about if my partner gets triggered when I had not meant to?" is your very good question. There is a simple answer. Do not follow on from his or her response. Instead, *step back and explain that you had not meant it like that.*

Imagine an argument being like two boats that keep bumping into each other... You trigger (involuntarily) and that's the first bump, then your partner responds, if you start from their response and keep going in that direction, you are in for a bumpy ride. If you step back, you are in for some smooth sailing.

Example?

Tom: "Hey, Mary, you have not posted the letter yet."

Mary: "I have been working all day, what have you been doing?"

Tom: "I have been looking for a job, why do you make me feel guilty about it?"

…Bumpy ride for the next 30 minutes.

You see, Tom triggered and then replied to Mary's response "what have you been doing?" But that question really did not want an answer, did it? The real function was to vent Mary's frustration…

Let's wind it back then:

Tom: "Hey Mary, you have not posted the letter yet."

Mary: "I have been working all day, what have you been doing?"

Tom: "No, Mary, I didn't mean to accuse you. Just noticed and I was asking if you wanted me to post it…"

Mary: "Sorry I misunderstood, thanks, if you can…"

…Smooth sailing and candlelit dinner in 30 minutes then…

The only issue with this example is that people don't use paper mail anymore, but sure you can see that if you catch things at this early stage, you can literally turn a potentially painful situation into a nice experience.

But what happens when the trigger comes to you? What happens if it is actually meant? The best way is to *defuse the trigger*. There are three ways you can do this:

1. *Ignore the trigger,* walking away pretending not to have
   heard it is quite good but if you do it repeatedly it may get on

your partner's nerves, depending on her/his personality and if s/he has a bone to pick with you.

2. *Take it as a joke*, this may be risky. If it is involuntary, then usually things get sorted immediately, but if it isn't your partner may take it as a challenge, like, "S/he doesn't even take me seriously!" It also depends on the importance of the topic...

3. *Explain expressing your feelings,* which is the hardest but best and safest response. Something similar to what we have learned already, like, "I understand you are annoyed but please understand that I am very tired too now," and then add a suggestion or an "action point" as businesspeople like to call them: "Shall we talk about it after dinner when we are more relaxed?"

This usually gives the other partner the chance to think about the *real issue* (not the trigger, remember?) and you can turn what would be a useless and unpleasant row into a chance to talk something over constructively.

However, if you say, "Let's talk about it later," then do... Do not use it as a "get out trick" – even if the temptation is big...

In conclusion, ***if you need to respond to a trigger, defuse it, if you give a trigger by mistake, explain that you did not mean it.*** This will do the trick in most cases.

Try, if you can, and especially as you become more experienced at managing these situations, to stop the argument at this stage. At this stage, in fact arguments are mainly a matter of "getting on each other's nerves", which is unpleasant but manageable. It is in the next stage, however, that things start to become personal...

De-escalating an Argument

Escalation is the longest part of the argument, and it is the one before the tipping point. So, in a way, it is very unpleasant and as we have just said things start to become painful and personal during escalation. On the other hand, the trigger and first response are usually a matter of seconds (even less than one second!) How about if you are caught off guard, or simply you couldn't defuse the trigger?

Then, the good news is that the next phase is longer, and this gives you more time to try to change it. And the way to change it is by *de-escalating.*

First of all, you need to understand that **to de-escalate an argument you must avoid getting caught in all its twists and turns.** What do we mean? We have the tendency to answer all the points, all the questions, all the challenges. It's like being on Twitter. And that is useless, tiring, and bad for your relationship. We feel like we are at a football game or basketball game and we need to score as many points as possible.

The reality is that this very fact leads us away from *the real goal which is to avoid a useless argument (or match), avoid pain and hurt and protect your relationship.* Who cares if it was really you who forgot the keys 3 years ago when you got locked out? And if it was? And if it was your partner? What would change? The only thing that changes is that *by bringing unpleasant and conflictual topics up you strain your relationship, and you suffer.*

So, keep the eye on "the big prize" rather than on all the crumbs that lead to the tipping point. Keeping this in mind, here is what you need to do.

Listen to your partner

We tend to interrupt each other in arguments and a clear sign of escalation is increasingly frequent and faster interruptions. This in itself becomes annoying and a cause of frustration etc....

So, listen till your partner has finished and you will have already reduced the *tension in the argument.*

Agree when possible

Because we have been triggered, we already start every exchange with the "no, you are wrong, and I am right" attitude. Well, that is a recipe for disaster. Instead, try the exact opposite. I know it is hard and our egos get in the way with these things but try to use sentences like these as far and as often as possible:

"I agree..."

"I can see your point."

"I had not seen it from that perspective."

Even

"I am not sure, but I will think about it."

If you feel like doing it just to defuse the argument, please go ahead...

Allow your partner to chill down

Take time before you reply. Who said that you need to answer straight away?

Then again, on some points you may want to give your partner a chance to "ramble on a bit". You see, jumping from point to point is very stressful and tense. Elaborating on a point instead is more relaxing.

Be careful which point you pick; choose one that is not too sensitive, not very confrontational and literally sidetrack your partner saying, "Can you explain this a bit more?" You see, this way you will give your partner a chance to "breathe"...

The best chances are when s/he brings into the argument a third person (not present of course!) like "When I saw Charlie he was still walking back on foot and his car was broken and you told me..." Stop him/her there (not verbally, just ignore the "and you told me and ..." and anything after that) and say, "Tell me more about Charlie's accident that night."

This way you show interest, you divert in another person and you also give your partner a chance to cool down, on a less emotional topic.

Express your feelings!

You have already seen the power of expressing feelings... Now, it is hard to do it during an argument, but if you do... This is the most disarming tactic you can have.

Arguments are based on the "being right or wrong" plane... They are structured around rational, not emotional points. Arguments don't start with sentences like, "When you said I was stupid I felt really hurt inside..." (emphasis on feeling) but, "You even told me that I am stupid!" (meaning, "Admit you are wrong, I am not stupid!").

So, if you can, do bring in how you are feeling about the argument. Do it without shouting and try to be as calm but sincere as possible. Also *do not express your feelings like an accusation.* Avoid saying, "you". Use sentences like:

"At this stage the conversation is becoming painful for me."

"These are things that are upsetting me very much."

"I am not ready to talk about painful things in this situation"

Even give warnings like:

"I am not sure if we go on like this that I can bear it much longer."

But at all costs avoid sentences like:

"You are hurting me now!" That's an accusation.

"What you say is very painful."

It does take time to de-escalate an argument. You may end up talking for a while, but keep calming it down rather than "sparking it up."

In most cases, *after a few minutes of de-escalation you will notice your partner has started collaborating with it.* Incredibly enough you only need to "hold the fort" (of peace of course) for a few minutes and your partner will come back to his/her senses.

At that stage, s/he will realize that what was about to happen was too painful and start giving soothing topics, ways out... the first joke is always the best sign ever that the argument is fully and finally over!

Walk away

Yes, Namina was actually right. If everything fails, walk away. When you have no other option, physical distance may be your only one. If your relationship is quite "argumentative" this may well be all you can do to start with. Later on, you will be able to de-escalate or even defuse the trigger. Don't be ashamed if this is all you can do.

High five to you too; it is always wise to avoid the tipping point. In fact, it may send your partner the message that s/he has gone too far. Walking away is a clear boundary setting signal. And in relationships sometimes boundaries are necessary

But if you can, **try to walk away calmly.** Explain why, with sentences like:

"Sorry, this is becoming too much, I need to take a break."

"I really can't manage this anymore, I need some fresh air."

If you can, **stay away for at least 20 minutes.** That's the time it takes for people to cool down... If you approach him or her earlier, you may re-ignite the argument.

Finally, **follow up with a friendly chat**. And there is one thing you should not forget in this: tell your partner that your walking away was not personal but because of the tension of the situation. This is your message. The "solving problems" conversation can (and maybe should) happen at a later stage. This is primarily to explain your reaction.

Moving onto Sunnier Beaches

This has been a tough chapter, I apologize. I understand that these are painful topics, but I had to discuss it in full, I hope you understand me... But now we can all breathe a sigh of relief and what makes me happy is that now you can solve even quite problematic situations! You must be quite relieved, as – you know, now you can avoid most arguments, which takes away a lot of insecurities and anxiety.

But before we move on, two little tips...

In any follow up to the (hopefully missed) argument don't be afraid to say "sorry." This beautiful word can literally disarm anybody and defuse any sticky situation. It is also very cathartic, very liberating...

After any (hopefully missed) argument have some bonding, some quality time together... Like after any problem you face – *relationships need constant nourishment...*

But now onto new beaches... And some may well be very new to you indeed! What do I mean? Well, you'll have to read the next chapter to find out...

7

MODELING YOUR RELATIONSHIP

L et me introduce you to some friends of mine. Their names are Lisa and Geoff. They have been together for a long time now. They are not married, but they have been living together for some time. And yes, they live in a flat on the suburbs. Unfortunately, so they say, they have two cars, because he works as a clerk on one side of town while she works as a teacher on the other side of town.

So, as you may expect, they have busy professional lives, but they do spend their weekends together. Their plans? Well, the main one for this year is to have a "proper holiday..." Disappointed? Did you expect the tapping of tiny feet? Er... maybe in the future; it's not off, but you know... it's a big choice.

But did I mention that I also have friends a few miles off in the countryside? They live on a hill and they set up their organic farm there. They have been doing it for some years now. It was hard at first, and it still is. But they are now seeing the fruit of their work. To start with, what used to be barren land is now a forest.

Of course, they live together and work together, and they are in a relationship. Their names? Ah, sorry, I was forgetting, Paul, Miles and Frank...

Can you help me now? I need to know what sort of challenges the two "groups" have, what their relationships may be like, what are the differences etc.... While you are at it, you can even think which you would like best... Don't need to tell me, just for you... I'll be out on the balcony if you need me.

...

It was a bit windy outside. Now have you compared the two relation-ships? Sure, you can see that one is turning into what we may call a *traditional relationship.* It is heterosexual, it is a couple, they live together, they have a "normal" life and "normal" plans. By "normal" we mean "common". In psychology and sociology normality has a different meaning from what people usually intend. Yes, I *am* teasing you and yes, it is a theme of this chapter.

Looking at my countryside friends, you can't have missed that there are three of them in the relationship, and that is fairly unusual (not that much, really). You will have noticed that it is a homosexual rela-tionship and that is not "canonical".

On to their challenges now... Remember that this is a "mind experiment". I think we will agree that from what we have seen,

Lisa and Geoff are already dealing with pressures from work, social life and urban living. Tom, Miles and Frank on the other hand may be facing a bit of prejudice. They are not the kind of relationship the local villagers are used to seeing at church on Sundays. And of course, living and working together has its disadvantages.

But have you also considered that having a *polyamorous relationship* also means having possible problems and even few role models and past examples to go by? It's actually quite hard...

So, what can we learn from this thought experiment?

- *There are many relationship models, some common and some not.*
- *Each has its internal dynamics but also challenges.*

And this is really what this chapter is all about. We have seen how relationships change with time; now we will see **archetypal models that you can use to shape your relationship on**.

Having said this, you can be creative, mix models, and take a bit from one and a bit from the other... You don't need to follow each model exactly; relationships are not flatpack furniture with instructions to follow in detail...

Relationships and "Normality"

Today you are going to meet lots of my friends. Martha and Stewart are a couple from the Midwest. He works in a bank and she stays at home, minding the children and doing charitable work. They are not married but they are very happy together. But I made a mistake... They *were* a couple from the Midwest in the 1950s!

You see, what appears "normal" now was totally unacceptable some time ago. A lot depends on where you live, but to take the average US provincial town, even an interracial couple would have been "taboo" just a few decades ago (I suppose it still is in some places) ...

What does this tell us? That *"normality as we mean it is a cultural construct".* It does not exist; in fact, it keeps changing. It depends on *the traditions and values of a community.* In fact, what is normal in some northern European countries and has been normal there for decades sounds "outrageous" or "futuristic" (depending on your approach) to most people in the USA nowadays.

So, psychologists and sociologists do not like to use the word "normal". Normal in fact means "adhering to a norm", which is a rule, a law. And the only "norm" that matters to psychologists and sociologists is that people are happy and that they do not do any harm to other people with their behavior.

So, three or even twenty people living a relationship who are happy with it and bother no one else are perfectly "normal" from a psychological or sociological point of view. And here, we use the word "normal" as "acceptable".

No relationship is the same. But this "normality myth" tends to make them all the same. It puts limits that are often a barrier to the partners' own happiness. In the Western World and also some Asian society it is becoming more "permissive". By this we mean that it is more "accepting of people's personal choices".

Therefore, things that were normal and expected just not long ago are now no longer so. For example, a married couple was expected to have children in the first few years of their marriage. Now, because children "cost" and because society in general has become less strict, this is no longer expected.

But it's also true that some rules were (are valid) for some people and not other people. We mentioned polyamory... It's nothing new though... Not if you were a European king... As a poor person you would have been hanged or burned on the stake or whatever if you had an affair. On the other hand, kings were expected to have "concubines" and they actually lived with the King and the Queen, went to their parties and were literally paid for their services from the royal purse.

So, here you see, this "normality" has always had differences... Yet again, while we look at the European aristocracy (noble people like dukes, counts, and barons) as "traditional and conservative" they too have always had a very open and relaxed attitude towards extramarital affairs and even homosexuality. Only among their class though. Apparently, the poor "could not manage such things" and had to be deterred and even convicted for them...

We will see that all the "models" in this chapter are not at all new. We should not see the modern world as being "the most liberal" when it comes to relationship. It is not necessarily so. For example, an Ancient Greek man was expected to have a wife and a male lover. Expected by the age of 9 – the boy lover, I mean.

On the other hand, in the "cradle of democracy", Athens in Ancient Greece only 25% of people were actually considered "humans" or "people" as the other 75% was made up of women and slaves, both regarded and treated as animals and property…

What I am saying is that things are not "linear" in history and "progress" is not one directional. They are multifaceted and complex instead. But we can also find examples of "modern relationship models" in the old days…

Taking the US as an example, statistics show that 64% of people are really happy with their relationships. The worrying data is 19% of people who are in some ways not happy with it, according to a survey by eHarmony. This is quite a lot, in fact.

But there is good news too. In a study by Perelli-Harris, Hoherz, Lappegård and Evans the results show that married people in the UK, Australia, Germany, and Norway are on the whole happier than people who are not in stable relationships. This is based mainly on midlife people, but it shows that relationships on the whole have a positive effect ('Mind the "Happiness" Gap: The Relationship Between Cohabitation, Marriage and Subjective Well-being in the United Kingdom, Australia, Germany, and Norway' published in *Demography*, August 2019).

Being Comfortable with Your Relationship

But we skipped on the most important point ever: *to be happy in a relationship you need to be comfortable with it.* That little word, "comfortable" is the key to everything. It is the *foundation of all relationships.* Both partners (or more) need to be comfortable with it.

One of the reasons why many relationships break up is adultery. Now, if the couple is comfortable with one (or both) having an external relationship, a "lover", then it's all fine. The problem arises when one of them is not comfortable with it. Even here, habits are different according to class in the West. Rich entrepreneurs live in a social milieu where having "lovers" is normal. It is quite common for both partners to have extramarital relationships and to be open about it. It is much less accepted in middle- and lower-class couples though.

So, *it is not up to the sociologist or the psychologist to tell you what you should be comfortable with. It is up to the psychologist and sociologist to help you reach that level of comfort that will make your relationship successful*.

This is very important because we need to understand your role and my role in this chapter.

I will offer you a wide range of models, to consider, play with, tweak etc. But the choice must be yours. I cannot tell you which one is the best relationship model for you. And use this word as your guiding light: "comfortable".

You won't need to tell me. You know I am like the elf you keep locked in a draw... Silent and discreet. But then my job is to help you make those changes to your relationship so that you have a model that you feel comfortable with.

And being comfortable with the structure and dynamics of your relationship is the best way to avoid anxiety and insecurities.

Modeling or Molding Your Relationship: Key Concepts

Even before we look at some models and their issues (and advantages, why not?) we need to see some principles.

Model consensually

You cannot add or change aspects of your relationship without the consent of your partner(s). This is why many extramarital relationships spell the end of the relationship... They are carried out behind the back of the partner...

But even with small changes, you need to make sure that your partner is happy with them. If you want, for example a more "friendly" relationship (wait and see), then you must make sure you both are comfortable with it.

Work together

Collaboration is key to all relationships and it follows from consent. What matters is that any change you want to bring to your relationship is tackled as a collaborative task. Take it as a "shared project". This alone will strengthen the bonds of your relationship.

Pause and reflect

Don't go full steam only to find out that "it wasn't like you had expected" ... Take things slowly and take regular pauses to reflect (together!) on how things are actually working out for both of you.

Be ready to step back and change plan

If things are not working out, fine. Don't feel that "you have to finish what you have started". You should be ready to go back to how things were before. Maybe you can try it another time, later on? Maybe it was just a bad idea! It does not matter. Your key aim is to be – remember? – *comfortable* with the changes!

Archetypal Relationship Models

What follows is not a series of rules or rigid structures. On the contrary. Like being a "mother", "teacher" or "friend" is a general idea with some key qualities, but it allows for a wide range of shades and realization in practice, the same applies to an archetype.

Archetypes are key anthropological concepts. For example, we have the idea of tyranny or democracy in politics, but then there are many different types of tyrannies and democracies. So, read what follows as "general overall types", which is exactly what archetype means.

Some are common nowadays and some less.

The Married Couple

The most widespread "mold" for relationships is the "married couple". Until recently, and still in many countries, this mainly stands for a "heterosexual married couple". However, this very archetype is changing in very liberal countries like Sweden and Denmark.

It is also true that with the introduction of LGBT weddings or civil partnerships in many countries, LGBT couples have embraced the values and dynamics of the "married couple". In many cases the life-style of a gay married couple is very virtually the same as that of a straight married couple. And this is what matters from the point of view of relationships.

There are some great advantages to this model:

- Stability over time
- Legal protection
- Financial protection
- Easy recognition and acceptance by society and the community
- Religious choice (especially if straight)
- Strong legal protection for children

On the other hand, it is quite demanding too. In fact, it requires:

- Long term commitment
- Usually (exceptions can be found!) a faithful and monogamous lifestyle
- Intensive relationship
- Lack of freedom in case you wish to change – a divorce has big legal, and practical consequences and it takes time. In some countries and cultures, divorce is not even accepted.

This gives you a clear idea that when you want to mold your relationship into the "married couple" model, there are big considerations to make. But it is also a good starting point to show you that this modeling of relationships needs consensual partners, collaboration, and some deep thinking.

And this is true even if you do not want to institutionalize your choice.

The Same or Different Culture Relationships

These are two models, one opposite to the other, and we shall see them together. Having a partner from your own culture is usually easier and this is the reason why most people choose this route. Moreover, society makes it very easy.

On the other hand, sharing a life with someone from a different culture can be fascinating and a wonderful experience. This, in successfully well integrated cases, ends up mixing the two cultures. However, the cultural difference usually remains to some extent and it can cause frictions all through the relationship.

A key issue is the language. Usually, people choose the language of the place where they live as their main language. But then there is the challenge of which language(s) to speak with the children, when and why.

It is quite common that the partner who does not live in his/her culture will want to preserve his/her culture with the child or children. This will mean communicating in a language that others do not understand. This can also cause conflictual situations with the partner.

The Friendly Relationship

I have been waiting to talk to you about this for a long time. In most romantic relationships there is also *a strong element of friendship.* We have seen how when this is true, the ex-partners often (not always) find it easier to keep good relations after breaking up.

People who become romantically attached after they have been friends for long usually preserve this friendly element. And this can continue and even grow all through the relationship.

This has some beautiful traits:

- Shared activities
- Shared views
- A sense of complicity
- Playfulness
- Mutual support
- Adaptability and flexibility within and with the relationship

However, not everybody finds the "friendship/intimate" distinction easy to manage. Some people for cultural reason do not see friends as people to have an intimate relationship with. Macho men who see friendship mainly as an "absolute denial of one's own sexuality" kind of bond, where playing darts or talking football are based on the mutual understanding that there cannot even be a sexual thought between them... Well, you get the picture... People with this cultural idea of friendship will find it hard to be friends with their sexual partner.

And this means that if the relationship becomes friendly oriented, these people may find having intimate moments "weird" and "uncomfortable". "Like having sex with my best friend," is the usual sort of phrase they will use to describe how they feel.

On the contrary, there are people who are quite fluid with the sexual/friendly dimensions. If that is your kind of person and your partner is similar, then you will find it easy to introduce more of a friendship into your relationship.

If you choose to add a "friendship element" to your relationship though do it "playing games". This is how friendships naturally develop: through shared activities with a bonding element. Instead of saying, "Now we have to behave like friends," do things that friends usually do together and you will naturally start behaving like friends.

Nice trick, isn't it?

The Polyamorous Relationship

This is quite a complex topic, but polyamory and metrosexuality are becoming more and more popular, or maybe they are just surfacing now after decades if not centuries of repression. We said that these were both expected, not just accepted in Ancient Greece. But of men, not women! That was more than a bit unfair.

Similarly, in some Arabic countries polygamy is perfectly legal. Again, if you are a man and you want more than one wife. Not if you are a woman though.

The dynamics of this sort of relationships however are very, very complex. They are not impossible by any means, but you need a very open attitude towards relationships. There is also the risk of jealousy within the relationship. So, **absolutely *key* to polyamorous relationship is excellent, constant, honest, and open communication.**

There are whole books about it now. If this is where you are going, this very book has too wide a scope to deal with polyamorous relationships in detail. It's like bringing up a child... A huge learning curve. So, I would suggest that if this is where you are heading or if you want to experiment with it and you are new to polyamory you should:

- Read specialized books about it (check in the reading list at the end of this book).
- Maybe try with experienced people first.

If you are in a monogamous relationship and to wish to bring a third into it (or another couple etc.; the number is not the point), then make sure your partner is fully happy with it. Also make sure that you two take responsibility for the progress and happiness (and integration) of the third.

You see, in this case, you would be the "majority" to start with. But then again, make sure that the newcomer(s) does not try to split you two up. Unfortunately, there are actually people who derive pleasure from splitting other couples up. Of course, a couple wanting to introduce another partner can be an inviting situation for these people.

But I don't wish to worry you, scare you, or prejudice you. This, as we said, is a very complex and delicate process. You will find yourself navigating very narrow straights, but if this is what makes you happy...

- read a lot about it,
- talk to specialists,
- join groups that share experiences,
- take it slow.

And of course, good luck! It can be an almost magic journey.

The Intermittent Relationship

There is the time factor too to consider. Who said that all relationships need to be continuous? I personally have friends who have a relationship with people they only meet once in a while, usually regularly, but then each goes to his/her home and they meet again maybe a month later.

This is also quite common with young relationships. Sometimes partners only meet at the weekend and they keep separate all week. For people in their teens or in their twenties, this is a very common type of relationship.

It is fairly convenient from many points of view.

- You don't need to share daily stress, often during working days. That, remember, can be a heavy strain on any relationship.

- It is long term but not intensive.
- It suits a wide range of commitment level. This type of relationship where you can be fully committed to each other or just experimenting with each other.
- It gives each partner his or her private space and time.
- It's a good stage in between "dating" and "going steady".
- It can be a good compromise when the relationship is facing trouble instead of "taking a break". It can be that, "we are still together but we also want time on our own individually to think things over".
- It can work to keep the "infatuation" and attraction alive.

However, in many cases, these relationships don't last in this form for too long. I do know some that have gone on for years... But this is also an "in between stages" type of relationship. Also, it often happens that one of the two partners wants to "move to the next stage", which means "having a closer and more committed relationship".

When this happens, the other partner may accept, even enthusiastically. But sometimes s/he won't. Losing that freedom, the time on your own etc. can be deterrents. And any increased commitment can find people unwilling or not ready for it.

In this case, maybe you can try to reach a compromise and propose an experiment. Take it gradually and, for example, if you meet a weekend every month, instead of jumping straight into the "let's move in together" phase, meet twice a month instead... Easing the less willing partner into the new situation is a good strategy and it will also give both partners a chance to become comfortable with each other.

Painting Your Relationship

Thus, we have seen a series of archetypal relationships. There are also others if you wish, in fact we said that every relationship is unique. The fiery relationship for example (those "love-hate/fight – make peace" kind of relationships) or the super passionate one. These, however, are not models you can choose rationally. You are far more likely to choose one of the archetypes we have seen when a "thunder and lightning" relationship is calming down and you may be looking for it to take a more "sustainable" shape...

The fact is that I would invite you to take these archetypes not as "boxes in which you can put your relationship" but as *a palette of colors to use to paint your relationship so that you are comfortable with it and it suits your needs and wishes"*.

There is no reason why you can't have elements of a friendly relationship with elements of a steady "married couple" relationship working perfectly together. And you can even have the commitment of a married couple kind of relationship and the freedom of an intermittent relationship or even a polyamorous one at that and the cocktail can be perfectly fine.

Whatever you choose, however, remember that **this is your relationship with your partner, not with society**. As long as you two are consensual and harm no one, society has no authority to tell you what sort of relationship you should have or how to manage it.

The lesson to take home is that *if you are not comfortable with a relationship you will feel anxious and insecure about it, but there are many models of relationships and you can use them to mix and shape the one you feel most comfortable with.*

And here we close with that beautiful word, "comfort" … in fact, the next chapter will be about switching comfortably from role to role within your relationship, an art that needs some social but also linguistic skills.

8

LACK AND FEAR OF INTIMACY

Intimacy is so important to relationships that we need to spend a few more words on it…. We looked at the "normal", if you want "general" and even "positive" side of it in the previous chapter… But now we need to enter a more problematic area…

I guess you remember when I mentioned the "chance" of having a relationship with little or no intimacy within it. It was fairly acceptable in the past; kings and queens often had little real intimacy; their relationship in many cases was a "state matter" – nothing to do with love and intimacy.

We come from a long history of "practical needs and solutions in relationships". Even if kings and princes were an extreme case, there was often a good level of practicality even lower down the social hierarchy. Keeping the property together or extending wealth were an important consideration among the rich. But even the poor had to choose a partner that could help in the fields, at home, or with the little activity of the family.

But that in itself does not preclude the opportunity to establish a deeply intimate relationship. It just adds another layer of complexity to the relationship. Nowadays, in most rich countries, economic and practical considerations do have a role in these choices. However, they are not often an impediment.

So, how is it possible that some relationships may lack intimacy? Does it really still happen?

What Causes Lack of Intimacy

There is a huge range of levels of intimacy. So maybe we should first understand what we mean by "lack of it". There is no "prescribed" level of intimacy, but... ***There is lack of intimacy when one or more of the partners feel dissatisfied with the intimacy within the relationship.*** In simple words, it is subjective. If a couple hardly look at each other in the face once a week and they are happy with it... so are we! But if a couple for instance have lots of intimacy but one of the partners would like some more... then we have a problem.

Happiness is the key objective of psychology. But what may cause lack of intimacy? There are many reasons, for example:

- *Stress* on one or more of the partners.
- *Wellbeing issues, including mental issues.* For example, depression may lead to lack of intimacy.

- *Tiredness and lack of time.* When people work too much, for example.
- *Decreased affection and attachment within the relationship.* And this becomes a bigger issue, one which we have dealt with in many chapters of this book.
- *Intimacy avoidance*: this is, I am sorry to say, a psychological condition, and one which is hard to manage.

These may be the causes, and each has a different solution. Lack of intimacy, however, can be serious enough to spell the end itself of a relationship. So, in any case, **catch it early, at the very first signs.**

Wellbeing Causes and Solutions

We can group together stress, tiredness and other wellbeing problems as "wellbeing causes". We will exclude intimacy avoidance, because that is a specific condition, and we will see it later.

What can you do if this is the case?

First of all, you need to *assess the cause.* If there are sudden and/or big changes in your life patterns, if you know or notice that your partner is very tense, tired, despondent, lacking motivation etc. then you are onto something. This may be accompanied by a *decline in libido,* but not necessarily. Let's remember that intimacy is much wider than just eros.

If you know your partner well, you will find it easier to assess if it's a wellbeing issue. And then? Then you will have to act carefully...

- *Do not blame your partner.* He or she is not responsible, but a victim of some stressful situation. Sometimes we cannot hide the fact that we resent something from our partners. Try to avoid giving any sign of "blaming" him or her. Even the odd cynical word can really hurt in these cases.

- *Your aim is to aid in solving the root problem.* This is why you should avoid making it worse with your behavior.
- *Remember that your partner is vulnerable at this stage.* Be extra kind, therefore. When we are stressed etc., we do not have the same tolerance level as when we are relaxed.
- *Do not force intimacy and yourself onto your partner.* Though you may really want that big strong hug, try not to force it on your partner at this stage.

"Fine," you may say, "lots of things to avoid. But is there something we can actually positively do?" The answer is yes!

- *Boost your partner's confidence.* Double down on encouragements! "Well done!", "You don't know how much I love you...", "You are a pro!" etc. In all areas of life, try to add that extra sign of appreciation.
- *Have trials but choose your timing carefully.* Wait for when your partner is least stressed to try *some intimacy.* And this leads us to the next point.
- *Use "reduced doses".* You understood, maybe start with less intimate acts. Instead of the big hug and passionate kiss, start with holding hands for a short while, for example.
- *Check when your partner wants to stop and indulge him/her.* Don't take it personally if after only a few seconds

s/he wants to let go of your hand. It is not against you, but a personal matter. So, let go...

- *Slowly make your partner comfortable with intimacy again.* With well timed, even "scaled down" acts of intimacy, if necessary, patience and a bit of time, your partner will find intimacy more comfortable as time goes by... Then it will be downhill.

To give you an idea, it's a bit like getting a baby to like new food. If you give a toddler a whole big raw carrot and you insist every day the chances are that your child will hate carrots till the day s/he retires and beyond. If you give him or her a tiny, cooked slice with some sauce on it every now and then... Little by little your child will turn into a little rabbit. But above all...

Deal with the root problem. Of course, this may mean taking a holiday, taking counseling, changing life patterns etc. It really depends on what the root cause is. But while you wait for the big solution to come along (and it may take time), keep in mind the vulnerability of your partner.

It will take some time but *focus on progress,* and treasure any intimate moment you get...

Practical Causes and Solutions

There are practical causes too, like lack of time, distance, even financial worries can lead to a decrease in intimacy. Very often, the practical cause triggers a psychological reaction, and this then results in reduced intimacy.

Typical is work problems and financial insecurity. People lose self-confidence when things don't go well at work. Money worries can be really horrible. I hope you never have any, but if you have (had), you surely know what I mean. That anxiety can be literally debilitating. People with such worries sometimes find it hard to carry out quite common daily chores. Even personal hygiene can get overlooked.

And in fact, a sign that there are very deep issues is the lack of self-care. And this can appear at many levels from the way we dress, to combing our hair to untidiness at home and work. I don't mean people who are usually untidy... I mean unusual and increased untidiness.

Even eating disorders (small or big ones) can be caused by both emotional and practical problems. Binge eating is quite a common way of compensating for lack of confidence or excessive anxiety and worrying. Binge eating can also be a way of compensating lack of intimacy, tangentially. So, if you both end up binge eating, there is something you need to talk about...

The solutions are the same as the ones for psychological and emotional problems (wellbeing), but we can add a few tips...

- *Tackle the emotional and mental side of it first and independently from the practical side.* The practical side of it can take some time... But if you can improve the psychological reaction to them, you will open up doors to intimate moments.
- *Don't make your partner feel responsible for the practical*

problems. Ok, this is the same as with emotional problems, but it is worth reminding.

- *Take some time off,* if possible. This can be hard when there are problems, but even a weekend away from it all can work wonders.

Of course, here too, it is a matter of solving the root problem, in the long run. But the more you manage to have intimacy before that moment, the more your partner (and you) will have strength to wait till everything is sorted. You can even have a clearer mind, a better ability to solve problems if you take breaks from them... And even a stroll hand in hand in the park is a bit like meditating.

But now onto the tough one...

Intimacy Avoidance

Intimacy avoidance is actually a very serious psychological condition. There are, of course, many professional studies on the topic, by psychologists, psychotherapists, sexologists, and psychoanalysts. If you want to have an idea of the complexities of this condition, a fairly thorough explanation is in a chapter by Dr Magdalena Smieja from Jagiellonian University, Krakow, Poland, in the *Encyclopedia of Personality and Individual Differences* aptly entitled 'Intimacy Avoidance'.

This condition has been known and recognized for decades now, with studies going back to the 1980s. It can have **varying degrees and manifestations in real life**, but on the whole, it can be described as when *"an individual withdraws from emotional contact from a relationship partner."*

This is of course is a technical, generic, and above all abstract definition. But it means that a person is – to different degrees – uncomfortable with being intimate with the partner. And this is **not a phase, a temporary attitude, or a development**; it is actually a **steady psychological behavior.** If someone suffers from it, they don't do it with "him and not her" with one partner and not the other, at some stages and not others, when they are stressed and not when they are relaxed. They will do it, to some extent, in any intimate situation.

It's like when you have a phobia: you just have it, and you can't avoid it. Having said this, such avoidance can be worsened by stress, illness, practical problems etc. **Intimacy avoidance is, in fact, a syndrome.**

But how can you find out if someone suffers from intimacy avoidance? The *symptoms are many*, but they include:

- Feeling rejected.
- Feeling socially isolated.
- Feeling emotionally numb.
- Feeling emotionally engulfed.
- Having a constant need for approval.

These are fairly generic symptoms, true, but you may also notice a key behavior: **the person avoids situations that trigger emotions and feelings.**

This does not just apply to intimacy and intimate situations. Intimacy avoidance syndrome can reflect on everyday life. People who suffer from it are **very vulnerable individuals.** Over the years, they develop *strategies to avoid feeling emotionally vulnerable.* And that often translates in "not even getting near intimacy if possible."

Because intimacy and being emotionally engaged, alight or awake are closely linked, people with intimacy avoidance syndrome will try to avoid both.

In fact, *intimacy avoidance affects many areas of life:*

- *Intellectual life:* people with intimacy avoidance can find it hard to share their ideas with others (this can have serious repercussions on their career, academic progress etc.)
- *Emotional life:* as we said, these people avoid emotions, but they also find it hard to express emotions.
- *Sexual life:* this does not mean that they do not have sex, but that they will find it hard to live it as a "sharing experience" or to feel as free and engrossed as others, and especially to feel the full intimacy of the act.
- *Experiential life:* these people may find it hard to express how they experience the world to others.

In the long run, people with intimacy avoidance can *become disconnected with reality.* Especially mature people with this syndrome will have gone through so much frustration that they give up on connecting with reality.

What is more *people with intimacy avoidance syndrome often end up sabotaging their own relationship*. Sometimes people don't understand why their partner is actively undermining the relationship. It looks and sounds absurd. And yet quite a few people do this. They start off very well, but then suddenly it is *"as if they did it on purpose to ruin everything"*.

"Is it me?" the other partner may wonder… "Is there someone else and s/he does not want to tell me?" No, there isn't and sometimes, when there is someone, the "lover" is purely functional to ruining the relationship. You can ask yourself all the questions you want, and you will never get to the truth if you don't know what it is.

The person with this condition *wants intimacy with you*, but *also subconsciously fears intimacy with you*. Very often **they are too afraid of being abandoned that they cannot bring themselves to running the emotional risk of being intimate**. So, because they cannot break this psychological barrier, they ruin the relationship as a sad, really sad way out.

When they say, "It's not you; it's me," they actually mean it. But they cannot explain why they can't change or solve "their problem". Because it is too deep and subconscious. Their fear is too big and old for them to overcome. Sometimes they don't even know why they have it. Sometimes only mentioning it is too painful to even think about it. When we say "trauma" in psychology we actually mean a wound so deep and so painful – ok, I am getting tearful myself…

But then, *they also feel deeply guilty for ruining the relationship,* and the downward spiral keeps going deeper. It's really sad. You *need a professional.* Sorry if I stress this.

But it is also true that *some of us are instinctively attracted to vulnerable people.* People with intimacy avoidance syndrome ooze vulnerability. And if you are one of those who want to hug everyone with a sad glint in his/her eyes, the chances are you already have met someone with this syndrome or you likely will.

And *you will want to help. But you won't be able to on your own.* And that too can have consequences on your confidence, well-being, insecurities, present, and future relationship(s).

On one hand, this makes us treasure our emotional and intimate life even more... On the other it is a really serious and sad state of affairs. Lighter versions of the syndrome can be more manageable, of course, but heavier ones can literally ruin relationships and whole lives.

Intimacy avoidance syndrome requires professional help. I think you must have guessed it by now. I know that there is a stigma with these things, but really this is the only solution. Even in lighter cases, it is better to seek counseling on the matter. The condition can worsen later in life in fact.

But even if you will need counseling (even therapy, depending on the case) to get through it, there are ***coping strategies that the partners can adopt.*** And we will see them straight away after a little digression.

The question I have not answered yet is "what causes intimacy avoidance syndrome?" I am sure you may have a few ideas already, and I am also quite confident you got them right...

It is in fact one of those psychological problems that have their root cause in childhood. Now, if you like a bit of psychology you will know the "stereotypical Freudian explanation" ... the causes of adult problems must be sought in the early years of life... It is not always like this! There are many problems, even very common ones, that can pop up later in life; depression is a typical example (though it can have childhood roots too).

But you know one thing, I am sure: **when psychological problems originate in childhood, they are very serious indeed.** This is because *the trauma that causes these problems has worked its way into the subconscious.* What does it mean? It means that it provokes our behavior, our actions, reactions, and even feelings without us being aware of what is happening.

Imagine the pain and frustration a person goes through when s/he can't have a normal intimate life and cannot do anything about it. This explains why they may become detached from reality. One more reason to get a professional involved.

But what are these "childhood causes"? Even here, I am confident you guessed: *it often has to do with family or more generically the* *carers.* "This is turning into an episode of *Frasier,*" you must be thinking. And yes, intimacy avoidance syndrome has all the classic "psychology stereotypes you would find in a movie" kind of things...

"Anything more specific," you may wish to ask? Yes, there are some types of relationships with cares that are typically at the basis of this syndrome. Now I will tell you, and your eyes will get wet...

- *Aggressive carers;* yes, in many cases it is verbal or physical violence that cause this.
- *Dismissive carers;* in other cases, the carers do not show enough care and attention to the child.

There can be also other specific causes, like *the loss of one or more carers.* Finally, also *being abandoned by one or more carers* can cause a trauma big enough to cause this syndrome.

Cup of tea, little cry, and then we can resume...

...

Ok, this was not an exercise, but I thought that a little break to reflect would do us good. If it is in your nature to fall in love with vulnerable people, I am repeating myself, but I am doing it for your good – do not think you can do it alone, please. At the same time, do not think less of yourself for having sought professional help.

You see, that is the other side of these relationship... The "helping partner" is at high risk of disappointment or frustration:

- If s/he tries on his/her own and fails, that will be felt like a massive disappointment.

- If s/he seeks help then s/he may think, "I am not good enough."

The second statement could not be further from the truth... And... Now onto the good news!

While you wait for the counseling or therapy to show results, there is still a huge and important, but above all positive role for you in this situation. Do you remember the **coping strategies,** yes? Then here we go!

There are in fact, strategies for the helping partner but also strategies for the partner with the syndrome. And they can be – actually should be – approached as teamwork.

Strategies for partners of people with intimacy avoidance syndrome

For the "helping partner" there are a few tips that will help you cope with this very difficult condition.

- *Be patient*; this is very important. Understand that your partner will need time. Putting any pressure on your partner can actually make things worse (it is a source of anxiety).
- *Expect setbacks...* progress will not be perfectly smooth. There will be times when – it's just not working right now... - please be understanding and don't make your partner feel like s/he has failed or done something wrong.
- *Do not take it personally when your partner refuses intimacy.* These relationships have an awful lot of attempts, setbacks etc. But very importantly, when your partner says

"no" remember that it is not "no to you", but "no I can't and it's not your fault nor does it mean that I don't love you."

- *Do not react with anger when your partner refuses intimacy.* This is absolutely important. Any sign of anger will only push the trauma deeper into your partner's subconscious. This will make it more difficult to solve and it can even seriously worsen the condition.

- *Avoid surprises;* I know, you so want to book that trip and tell your beloved one over dinner! But that may make him or her feel "not in control" and that will trigger the syndrome. Instead, well, less like an episode of *Friends* but more realistic and, above all, comfortable for your partner... Plan the trip together.

- *Make small steps and clear, joint decisions;* this follows from the previous point. Discuss choices in detail and make sure that there is agreement on every point...

- *Make your partner feel in control.* Again, following from the previous point but applicable to all life choices together, even small ones like which shop to go to and which type of apples you want to buy.... The more your partner feels in control, the more s/he will be comfortable with intimacy.

- *Keep praising him/her and expressing your positive feelings towards him/her.* The praising is clear, but now imagine someone with intimacy problems living with someone who never expresses feelings... That makes it even harder, doesn't it? Instead, convey the idea that for you it is normal and beautiful to share feelings with him or her... This can be a game changer.

- *Make it clear that this is teamwork.* You will set out on a long journey together and if you live it together, if you manage it together, plan it together, share it etc., this very teamwork will make intimacy easier for your partner.

- *Listen carefully, without judgement and without pushing.* At some stage, your partner will want to open up about his or her traumatic experience. Here you need to be a bit like a professional counselor. Don't go like, "And who was he?" or "What happened next?" That looks and feels like you want to know their business. That's pushing him or her. No, instead! Just let your partner say what s/he wants, as s/he wants and as much as s/he wants. Your role is *to listen without judging and express empathy.* Do, say something along the lines of "I understand you," or "You must have suffered a lot," etc.

Strategies for people with intimacy avoidance syndrome

If it is you who has this problem… Above all, don't blame yourself. Ever! Even when those dark clouds come over your head full of examples of things you did wrong keep this light in mind: *you did not do it because you wanted it. You had to and this "thing" cannot be beaten alone.* No exception. Not even Superman can do it.

This being clear now we can look at a few coping strategies too. Your counselor will likely suggest the same, similar ones and even more, but a few to get you started…

- *Accept uncertainty;* things do go wrong, but then we can always fix them later. Playing sports can actually help you get comfortable with the idea. Especially a sport you are not good at. You know why? You will lose a lot. But you'll also get used to the idea that "losing ain't that bad after all!" It's just the matter of a moment...

- *Focus on day-by-day life.* A bit of planning is fine, but seize the day, live in the moment as far as you can. Too much planning shifts the focus into the future, which is uncertain, and uncertainties bring insecurities, and insecurities bring anxiety... You see where I am going.

- *Take on meditation or yoga*; these can be very good to relax and get in touch with your inner self, with your emotions and even face some of those gremlins we don't like too much.

- *Express self-compassion;* you need to be comfortable with yourself if you wish to become intimate with others. Compassion, however, is not just "pity" ... Do tell yourself "I was very unlucky with it," or even "That really hurt me." Fine, but then don't forget to say, "I felt really good about it," and "Look – what a beautiful person am I?"

- *Talk to yourself, tune into your inner dialogue*; don't be afraid to have long and especially honest conversations with yourself. Anything at all. From frivolous and trivial things to important ones. Above all, try to *tell yourself how you feel.* Some people even end up disagreeing with themselves and you know the good side of it? You can always choose to be on the winning side at the end.

- *Give yourself plenty of time.* Don't hurry, that only causes further pressure. It will take time, and you need to be patient.

But you also should not expect too much too soon from yourself. Take all the time you need.

- *Look at your past but take it slow*! If you are not comfortable with a thought from the past, don't dwell on it. In fact, this is better done during professional sessions. But if you do feel that there are a few episodes that you can recall now without being hurt too much, that you can cope with, and manage to recall, then give it a brief try every now and then. But do it when you have time, when you are calm, and especially when you feel good about yourself.

And we have come to the end of this very intense chapter. It was intense for me, so, I can imagine it was for you too. But this is the biggest, most difficult and complex problem we need to tackle in this book. And we have done it. Now you know that even serious psychological syndromes that can affect relationships very badly have a solution. Even if a professional one. But now you can recognize one, which makes all the difference...

In the next chapter we will change topic ("What a silly thing to say," you may think, but it's a clue, actually...)

So, take a big breath, relax, have a cup, of tea, and see you back when you are ready!

9

THE ART OF SWITCHING

•••T alking about changing topics, how many times during a single day does your relationship with your partner change? Let's be "imaginary voyeurs" for a second... We now have a camera fixed on the heads of two imaginary friends of mine: Aysha and Chris. At each stage, ask yourself what their relationship is like at that moment, and what has changed from before.

It is Saturday morning and Chris wakes up. Aysha is still in bed. But she needs to prepare breakfast for both. What is their relationship like now? When Aysha wakes up, breakfast is ready on the table and they greet with a kiss before they sit down. What is their relationship like now?

Chris is usually the one who reads the paper and talks about politics and the news, while Aysha tends to listen but she does not join in too much. What's changed in their relationship? Then, however, they need to wake up the children. This is quite a troublesome and often chaotic moment because the kids like to sleep, then they often argue over the bathroom turns... So Aysha takes a lead and deals with them while Chris makes himself scarce in the garden while checking on flowers and vegetables.

As it is Saturday, they then get into the car. Aysha has a driving license, but Chris does not. So Aysha drives to the shopping center, while Chris keeps the children quiet...

I could go on for the whole chapter, but I think it's enough to get the point. When they are in the car, for example, Aysha has a *leading role*, while at that stage Chris has a *backing role.* When Aysha wakes up the children, again she is the *leading partner* while he literally "gets temporarily out of the way" but still acts as a *facilitating partner.*

What we understand from this is that *roles within the relationship are continuously changing.* Chris and Aysha are not in the same *relative positions* at each change, and these changes can happen very quickly and frequently indeed.

And we have not even got through to lunchtime, let alone till Aysha and Chris go back to bed at night! Can you imagine how many times they need to *change roles during the day?* It can literally be hundreds of times. Each day. For a lifetime...

Now you understand why *being able to change and switch roles in a relationship is fundamental to its survival and happiness.* And of course, we are going to talk about it now.

Before we move on, however, I want to ask you one thing. If you have a partner, fine. If you don't choose the person you spent most time with during a whole day recently. You do know by now that I mind my business, so, instead of telling me, take a few minutes to think about part of a recent day and count the changes of roles you have had with him or her... The whole day would be far too long to consider. No need to tell me.

...

They were loads, weren't they? Then there is the extra factor that the more activities you undertake together, the more you need to switch roles. This does not happen just with partners. It happens in all sorts of relationships.

You know, once upon a time, people had more socially rigid roles and lives. What is more, especially in rural settings, they had fewer encounters during the day... It so happened that we started identifying people by only one single role in their lives. This was often the job or the provenance...

That's where we got names like Smith, Thatcher, etc.... But in the Twentieth Century we realized that everybody has a "range of roles and personalities". You are not the same person when you are at work or when you go shopping. Your role changes. At work you are a teacher, a builder, a nurse etc.... You have (or are) a boss and you have colleagues. You may even have clients, or patients etc.... But when you go shopping you are no longer a teacher or a nurse... You are the client now!

As you can see, we do this fluidly in many cases, but... There can be a few problems with partners.

Roles Within Relationships

While most roles are dictated by society, the same does not apply to relationships. We believe that we live in a free world... in some ways yes, but it's full of unwritten (or written) social rules.

When you meet a professional, there are rules of engagement... We all have that very respectful attitude towards medical doctors, don't we? When a police person stops you at the traffic lights, you take out your license and hope you don't get a ticket... When you board a plane, you listen to the captain and crew when they give you instructions about taking off etc....

These are all relationships with fairly *strict and pre-determined social rules.* But **in personal relationships social rules are looser, or sometimes they (almost) do not exist at all.**

This depends a bit on the society you live in. Not long ago in Western countries it was society that dictated which roles men and women had in their own personal relationships. This still lives on in many personal relationships, even if in softer version.

Example? There are still couples where some tasks are the sole domain of the woman, like cooking, doing the washing up, cleaning, and most house chores. That is a social rule, a legacy from times of old when women and men were not equal. This is still very common within couples of old people. It is very uncommon with young urban couples. But it does vary from place to place. While in New York or even more Copenhagen this would be very rare, in some rural areas of both the US and Europe, this type of "settlement" is still fairly common.

And we only looked at the US and the EU. There are countries around the world where these old rules are still written in law! But the reason why we are talking about it is another.

If there are pre-established social rules within a couple, the roles tend to be fairly steady. One partner will have one role most of the time, the other another role. These are usually a *leading role* and a *following role.* I used "following" rather than "subservient", "subdued" etc., because it's more general. But in some cases, we can talk about a *dominant role and a submissive role.* Where these definitions start is hard to say; as usual, it has personal and subjective perspectives too.

But when these fixed roles from the past do not exist, relationships become fluid and the two roles (with varying degrees, including middle ones) pass from one partner to the other... This means a lot of switching...

Ok, I am going to say it in very simple words: ***if you want a modern and free, egalitarian relationship you'd better be good at switching roles.***

You may think, "Fine, I am very good at it!" but the problem is that **both of you must be good at it and willing to do it.** In polyamorous relationships all members need to be good at this, and the dynamics can become very complex indeed.

Here is very often where problems come... A lot really depends on the past experiences of the partners. Now, let me tell you a story... Lisa and Paul have been partners for about one year, so they decided to move in together. They didn't want to get married straight away, you know...

Anyway, they moved in together and after a few weeks I got a call from Lisa... We met over a coffee and she told me that, well, things were not going as she had hoped. Why? Paul was totally "modern" when they were dating, "But indoors," she said, "he still expects me to be a "wife" in the old-fashioned way..."

I became curious and a bit worried, so I asked for some more details. They were not huge problems, but annoying enough to put a chink in their relationship. Basically, Paul does not like to cook, and that's fine with her in a way, but also, he does not help with the washing and washing up. They are only two things, but she is upset.

I have to ask for your advice here: why do you think Lisa is so upset? Why do you think that Paul has these "strange" habits?

...

Let's see... You may say that Lisa is worried that Paul will start with two or three things and then start withdrawing from other chores? Possible. Or that Lisa wants a perfect, "fairy tale" relationship, so any spot is incredibly annoying...

One thing though, equality cannot be such if there is just one unequal element... And this may be a matter of principle... You see, Lisa has a clear expectation of "equality across the board" and one or two things are enough to "remind her that she is not actually equal in Paul's eyes". And this can be frustrating, even very painful and it can "gnaw away" at a relationship in the long run.

But now I need your help once more. What about Paul? Why do you think he is behaving like this?

I take my coffee white with brown sugar if you're making it this time.

...

That was "the" perfect cup of coffee, thanks! Joking aside, what did you make of Paul? We may agree that he is not fully conscious of what he is doing. Surely, he does not understand that Lisa is anxious about it...

We may also agree that he has problems switching, doesn't he? And then we can try to guess why he is resisting this fully egalitarian settlement that Lisa is looking for. We may guess that there are some **cultural and experiential conditioning** in his behavior? This, in fact, looks very much like one of those "family traits" that come from years, decades even, of seeing your Mum or women in your family of origin doing certain things and not others...

Basically, we can expect that at his parents' home, Paul never saw his father do the washing up or anywhere near the washing machine... And it is *often the male partner who resists such egalitarian relationships.*

Imagine an extreme situation... Imagine a man who comes from a family where the male members have a very dominant position and female members are simply not treated as equals because of their culture and tradition... How easy would it be for this man to switch into an egalitarian relationship? Very hard indeed in most cases...

We will come back to this and give Lisa a helping hand in a minute, but first, something even more difficult...

Intimate Roles and Switching

So far, we talked about the washing up... Now, think how many different roles people can have when they are being intimate? Yes, that *includes sex...* Here the world of possibilities is huge. Depending of course on the tastes and preferences of the partners, but really there can be a lot of switching in these moments.

And maybe **the most "exciting" but also "frightful" switch is the one from "out of intimacy" to "into intimacy"**. You get my point...

This is in itself one of those moments when you get butterflies in your stomach and a flutter to your heart etc.... Very often there are **key signals, like gestures or words that indicate the willingness to switch into an intimate or sexual moment.** In the *Adams Family*, remember, it was when Morticia Adams spoke French... Ok, this is a funny take on it, but it does have an educational point; each couple has its own *"switching signals", and these often come from the history of the couple itself.*

In many cases these signals go back to the very "first time" of the couple, or at least to the very early stages of the relationship.

When these signals are given and not picked up, the partner sending them usually worries a lot. It is a "rejection" even if "coded" in a language that only the couple can understand. But there is no fooling the partner here. ***If you turn down your partner, always explain why.*** The "headache situation" is fine, as long as it is open and honest.

But think about this carefully; your partner will feel "rejected", even "embarrassed" and this can have huge consequences on his or her confidence. So, your "rejection" must be:

- *Calm*
- *Understanding and empathetic*
- *Specific in its reason*
- *Warm and not cold*

Something like, "Oh, sweetheart right now I have my mind on the electricity bill, I am sorry, I wish I could," then offer some **intimate compensation,** like a long hug, a cuddle etc.…

The "Oh, no, I have just done my hair," followed by standing up to light a cigarette is actually painful (and unhealthy!) You see, at this stage, ***your main goal is not to hurt your partner's feelings. Think about how you would feel about it!…***

Talking about which, what happens if it is your partner who turns you down? And how about if your partner does not behave as we just said? At worst, there's the "stop physical contact and move to something very cold and un-intimate" reaction. In this case, usually there is a serious problem within the couple, and it is time for a "relationship talk".

But in most cases the harm is done unconsciously. There are of course series of levels and reactions, from a simple "ignoring the sign but being sweet and intimate all the same" to "saying something that is too vague" etc.

Ok, here you need to approach your partner and have a chat about it. It is hard to say that you have been hurt. Especially on such intimate issues, there is a sense of humiliation and loss of face... But try to do it the very first time it happens, or as early as possible. ***Turning down offers of intimacy the wrong way cannot become a habit.*** That will start a really painful downward spiral that can ruin your relationship.

And, oddly enough, this is where you need to switch! Yes, you need to take on a *leading role* and start a conversation about what you expect of him or her in these situations. Now, note that you cannot say, "You cannot refuse my advances". That is not the point and make clear straight away that this is not where you are going. Doing this on its own will lower the barriers from your partner (s/he at this stage will be worrying about your "accepting the refusal" rather than the "how I did it was wrong").

Tell him that *the way s/he did it is hurtful.* Again, use the language of feelings we saw early on in this book: "When you stood up it hurt me, I expected a hug," or, "I felt bad because you didn't even tell me why you don't fancy it now..."

Don't be "nagging" but be firm on your right not to be hurt. It is not a confirmation but an "understanding each other moment". Basically, you need to teach him/her what you have just learned in this book. You too deserve a "rejection" which is calm, understanding, and empathetic, specific in the reason, warm, and followed by intimate compensation (a hug, a kiss, whatever...).

You will turn each other down over the years; this has to be done without hurting each other. So, both partners will benefit from learning this "switching out" skill.

Intimate, Personal and Social Roles... and More Switching!

While ideally most of us want egalitarian roles in social and personal situations, not everybody likes this in intimate roles. Pause, take a long breath and reflect. This is one of the weirdest balances to achieve in a relationship.

Do you know what I mean? Sheila and Frank are fully egalitarian. They have equal roles in the home, they share tasks with neighbors, they decide everything fully together, both work etc. But... When night comes and they cuddle on the sofa Sheila likes to feel protected and she cuddles within his arms...

So, at this stage, it is Frank who takes a leading role. This is a small and delicate example. But the fact is that *within the intimate sphere any consensual role is fully acceptable.*

One thing we need to understand is that being egalitarian and equal in the relationship does not, for example, mean having to have "egalitarian roles in bed". That is a different sphere where one partner may just want the other to take a leading role...

All rules apart from one are suspended in that sphere: *what you do must be consensual.*

Of course, these roles can be pretty wild. There has been a massive increase in fetish and S&M sexual activity in recent years... Things that were once "mythologically perverted" are now very common indeed. It is part of the ***process of sexual liberation*** that we have seen in the past decades (after the 80s in particular).

It has been brought about by pop musicians (Madonna being by far the biggest driving force of this revolution) and then with the advent of the Internet... We all know that things you didn't even know existed all of a sudden pop up in little (and may I say, quite insisting) windows out of nowhere...

Now sexual practices that only few knew existed in the past are within reach of young people as well... And in fact, that world has totally changed...

There remains the only untouchable rule here; ***all sexual acts and practices must be fully consensual.***

But apart from that, ***the more experimental sexual roles are, the more they require switching skills.*** There can be embarrassment, uncertainty and even confusion if the switch does not work well.

Having said this, it is not at all uncommon that the partner who has a leading role in bed may then have a following role out of it. There is no rule and when cheeky (nosy) people look at couples and "guess" what their intimate roles are, well, be aware that the way they behave in front of you may be totally different from what they do behind closed doors. But the key point would be that what they do behind closed doors is no one else's business...

What does a successful switch in these situations look like?

It is actually a very crafty skill. To be honest in the old S&M community they had clear rules... It's amazing how the whole world was perfectly regulated, with rules you would never break and even a form of etiquette. But that was a small and closely knit community. Now these practices have become more common, those rules have been forgotten.

Instead, I would actually stick to them very closely. They are all centered around **consent and safety** and they are designed to **make the transition from one role to the other smooth.**

- They are *very ritualized.* The ritual is usually always the same; there can be a dressing item, or words, or assuming certain positions etc. Usually more than one element together.
- *The leading partner starts this ritual.* The partner who takes the leading role in the sexual activity is also the one who "celebrates the ritual". Whether it is saying certain words etc., this is very important. It is the "easing in the following partner" that allows him/her to feel at ease and safe in this role.
- *There is always a way out for the following partner.*

Usually the partners establish "the word". It must be a word with no sexual reference, and if the following partner says it, the leading partner stops immediately, no questions asked. When you "lead" you may not be aware you are going too far. There is no option of disrespecting that word. In a way, it's the "thing" that keeps an element of equality even at this level. And when we say immediately we mean immediately. In fact, any act done after that is technically *non-consensual.*

- *The leading partner repeatedly checks for consent.* It is the good characteristic of a leading partner to make sure the following partner is actually happy. In "unequal sexual acts" the leading partner keeps asking the following partner if s/he like what they are doing. It's a responsibility, not just a "kinky game".

- *The switching out is slow, long and very warm and intimate.* There is a lot of cuddling, hugging, looking at each other straight in the eyes etc.... when moving out of the sexual roles and back into the personal roles. This too is very necessary to ease the transition into an egalitarian relationship. While the switching into can be quick, the switching out of can take half an hour to a whole day actually...

As you can see, there's a solution to everything. Relationships can be very complex, and we really need to be thankful to the people who developed a whole tried and tested, as well as safe process of switching in very intimate situations.

On a dry but necessary side note, this set of rules also safeguards both partners. Passing that line of consent means moving into "rape area". And in sex especially if one of the partners is "in control" we need to be doubly certain that that line is never crossed, not even by mistake.

When to Switch, How to Switch

Remember Lisa and Paul? I said we would come back to help them, and I always keep my word. Actually, you know I am lazy, and I am going to ask *you* to do it. But now we have to do two things...

- Remind ourselves of what Lisa and Paul's problem was.
- Look at this problem from a much deeper perspective we have now explored.

Let's start from the second (I like starting from the back) ... we have now seen that even very emotional switches, literally like that from S&M positions to equal partners (and even if you want to "boss and employee" – and have fun thinking that these are the exact opposite of what happens behind closed doors) *are* possible, and that *there is a tried and tested technique to do this switch.*

Now, from this perspective, Lisa and Paul's problem may look very small. Do you remember what it was? It was that Paul (for what we identified as cultural "legacy") would not do things like the washing up, and this, rightfully, gave Lisa the "feeling" that he did not see her as fully equal in the relationship.

Now we remember can I say one thing? By now I fully trust that you have lots of ideas on how to help her... So, can I absent myself for another cup of tea? Green tea now as coffee is bad for nerves...

...

Green tea is such a wonder of Nature... By the way did you know that it's excellent to lose weight? Turmeric tea in particular. It allows your body fat to turn from white fat to brown fat. White fat is the fat we store, brown fat is the fat we burn. Turmeric turns white fat into brown fat... On average, half a teaspoon of turmeric in a cup of water every day will make you lose 1.5 lb. a week. Not bad...

Enough with getting ready for summer though... What can we say about Lisa and Paul? For sure Paul needs to understand that "equality" has many practical implications. While this may look like a "little problem" compared with the "seismic switches" we have seen so far, it does not mean that the problem is less painful. What's more, Lisa may not want to address it because the "realization of the problem" is not huge, it may look "venial" and "petty" to "make a fuss" about such things.

Instead, what do you reckon? Should Lisa confront him about it? The answer is, I am sure you will agree, a resounding YES! And how should she do it? There are basically two options; one is like a diplomat trying to get a logical point across, the other is by tapping into Paul's emotional side and good will.

In practical terms... Most couples in this situation end up with one partner saying something along the lines of "It is my right that you...," or "You are not pulling your weight." The problem with this approach is not that it is factually wrong... It is that it puts the two partners into a conflictual situation... And whenever there is conflict there is risk of losing face, and when there is risk of losing face there is a defensive position... By now you know quite well that we are heading towards a confrontation at this stage...

Instead, can I suggest a different approach? It is different from what we normally would use (and fail), but familiar to us. Look at these sentences as examples:

"When I do the washing up and you don't help me, I feel as if you think it's a job I should do because I am a woman."

"When I do the washing, I would love to have a hand, you see, it is much harder than you think; you need to kneel down, pick up heavy clothes etc.... And they get heavier when you take them out to hang them."

That's a completely different approach from, "You don't help me with the washing because you think I am inferior," which may well be what one day Lisa will end up thinking and even shouting unless she sorts out this problem early on in her relationship.

Let's pause a second, though, because we have reached a very important point: **try to solve each problem in isolation in your relationship as soon as it arises or as soon as possible.** Trying to solve more problems in one go is usually disastrous. The discussion ends up jumping from one point to the other without solving a single one (it's called "kettle logic" by experts).

What is more, if the problem becomes ingrained, it is harder to eradi-cate and when you bring it up there is always the "Why didn't you bring this up before question?" Though it may be legitimate, this question shifts the focus from solving the problem to a series of memories from the past and accusations and it sets the discussion back...

But back to our main point; using the *language of emotions,* once more is the best chance you have to make a breach into your partner's heart and mind, and, at the same time, it is the best way to trigger a rational conversation aimed at a solution, and not at finding fault with each other.

Look at this like an hourglass: if you start accusing you will only get a defensive and irrational response. If instead you start by involving your partner and expressing your emotions, you will get the exact opposite: an open and solution oriented rational discussion.

Let's look back for a moment. We have made huge progress. Really... Look at how many problems and situations you can solve now. And because we are approaching the end of this book, we now want to turn to a very positive chapter... And I will leave you with an "exer-cise"... In your opinion, what makes a perfect relationship?

...

THE RECIPE FOR A GOOD RELATIONSHIP

A nd we finally reach a fully positive, sunlit, breezy chapter... We have gone through lots of important things in this book, from understanding the dynamics within relationships, to how to talk about sensitive topics to how to face critical moments... You have also met almost all my "imaginary friends" and you have seen that there are so many different situations in relationships that the world is your oyster if you take this positively.

Now we are coming to the end of this book, we can look at all the *ingredients you need to have a successful relationship.* But before I tell you my ideas, I would like you to brainstorm yours... As usual, take your time.

...

So, what do you think you need to have a good relationship? Most people come up with values, like "respect", and they are right actually. But there are also some practical ingredients, like communication skills, and we have seen how much they can make the difference between a successful relationship and an unsuccessful one.

So, without further ado, off we go!

Respect

Let's start with this. Respect is so fundamental in a relationship that we cannot ignore it, can we? One of the main anxieties in relationships is in fact losing respect, or "not being respected enough". Very often even betrayals are seen as "lack of respect".

But in many relationships, it also happens that *respect is taken for granted.* This can be fine, but I would suggest that **you keep expressing your respect to your partner and encourage your partner to do the same with you.**

If you mean it, say it! *Focus on your partner's positive traits and don't take them for granted;* if s/he does something good, praise him/her. Make sure your partner knows that you think highly of him/her...

You know by now that you need to **constantly feed your relationship**, and words and small gestures are "the food" of healthy relationships.

Honesty

Another quality that can make or break a relationship. "But surely no one wants to be dishonest in a relationship," you may ask? Well... Let's say that in most cases, *we start off with an idealized, fairy tale and idyllic image of what our relationship will be.* This is great, but in many cases this very "fairy tale idea of our relationship" is what ends up ruining it.

Example... George and Melissa started off a few months ago, and it was all perfect to start with. But after a while, things didn't look as perfect as they expected. Nothing major, really, a very small thing... Melissa likes playing chess and George went along with it. You know, when you are in the infatuation phase you like everything your partner likes. We literally have a "morphed" perception of reality. We actually really believe in ourselves that we like certain things...

But then the infatuation wears off and that more "realistic" perspective of reality comes back. But *we don't want to lose the "fairy tale idea of our relationship".* And it is because we want to preserve this ideal that we often start doing two little things:

- *Lying to ourselves*
- *Lying to our partner*

These little lies seem justified at first. We see them as white lies... But lies they are and in a relationship, they can have consequences. So, George rang me up the other day (they still have old fashioned telephones that "ring" in the world of imaginary friends) and he said that he can't face another long and boring game of chess, that he is a "physical person who likes being active, walking, doing sports, not sitting down for days on end in front of a chess board!"

I could smell a problem and so I asked a few probing questions... It turns out that George followed a very typical pattern...

- At first, he actually thought he would love playing chess.
- For a few months he was fine – he sort of enjoyed it.
- Then he started getting bored with it, but he *told himself that he would like it again very soon.*
- That "very soon" has never happened...
- He has not told Melissa about it and he is scared that if he does, their "perfect relationship won't be perfect anymore."

You see, the first lie to oneself actually makes it hard to then be honest with the partner. But as you can notice it all happens perfectly innocently... but then you end up with a "secret" from your partner... And that's a problem. George hasn't lied to Melissa, but he is holding a secret...

Guess what I told him?

...

You guessed; I told him to come clear as soon as possible. You cannot bottle something up or it will end up coming out at the worst possible time (years later during an animated argument – so, it comes as a "weapon" and not as a solution).

He can always play some chess with her, of course, but he needs to be honest, with himself and with Melissa. He needs her to understand that *he has not fooled her by pretending that he liked chess.* This is a problem he correctly has. He needs to be very clear and tell her that he actually did enjoy it at first but now he just does not...

Then there will be practical steps to take (e.g., she will need someone else to play chess with etc.), but the point is that **you need to be vigilant about situations where you "hide a small thing" from your partner.** This may lead to more and more hiding and a downward spiral.

So, keep an eye on the small things and you will keep your relationship clean shining with honesty.

Flexibility

We spent a lot of time talking about how relationships change. But I want to look at this from a new perspective. Now, there is something that people would define as "magic" when a new relationship starts. Those moonlit nights and strolls in a park full of scented flowers are inebriating...

And we hold onto those moments with great fondness, but also with the worry that if the relationship changes, those moments will never happen again. It is the "fairy tale" image we talked about in the previous section... That very ideal image can be an obstacle to flexibility.

When things are perfect, we don't want to change them. The problem is that even when they are no longer perfect, we don't want to change them and if we do, we want to "change them back", not adapt them to the new situation.

That is not flexibility; that is nostalgia.

You should fully enjoy that fizzy and aromatic feeling you have during the infatuation phase. But please consider this: ***there isn't just one fairy tale, there can be many, and many beautiful stories too.***

I'll explain, the fact that the first phase will come to an end is inevitable. But instead of seeing it as "the end of a fairy tale" look at it as *"the beginning of a new story"*. Maybe you have matured, and it won't be a fairy tale, but there are wonderful novels for adults too, full of passion and happiness...

Shared Values

This is one of the foundations of good relationships. Most of us, at least adults, look for a partner with the same value system as we have. A left-wing person will look for a left-wing partner; a vegan will hardly get on well with a butcher. You know what I mean...

"But hold on, there are couples who even have different religious beliefs!" You are right! In some places they are even fairly common, especially big melting pots like Paris or London. But there is one key thing they share: they have a religious or spiritual belief... That alone is a strong bond.

These couples have to negotiate impressive cultural and moral variables to be honest. Different traditions, holidays, often even languages... But religions have much more in common than most people believe. The core value system of a Christian, Buddhist, Muslim, Jew, Sikh, Hindu, or even an Animist is very similar. But there are of course lots of "challenges".

Having said this, records show that multicultural and multi-faith couples do work very well. Maybe the fact itself of having to find an agreement on very important and intimate topics makes them very strong indeed (and flexible at the same time)!

Once you have managed such a huge step, you certainly are ready to face the world with lots of confidence.

It is actually more difficult to find an agreement between an atheist and a believer, of *any* religious or spiritual persuasion. Usually, atheists and agnostics stick together and so do believers. But again, this is not a strict rule.

But in any case, *shared values and beliefs are a strong bonding element within couples.*

You don't need to share absolutely all values, but a large section of values is really fundamental for a couple. To start with, you will avoid never-ending arguments (trust me on this!) You will also have a shared mission in some cases. A couple who loves animals can work together for charitable work or on campaigns for animal rights, for example...

If you "activate" your shared values, these activities can too become "food for your relationship". What is more, they will do a lot to preserve or increase mutual respect and esteem.

Independence

Once upon a time, women would get married and lose any independence. That wedding day was the beginning of a life where the husband provided for food, shelter etc. and the wife took her "role" as dependent on him.

This still happens in some cultures, but it would be totally unacceptable to most modern women. The fact is that if you fully depend on one partner, you will lose a lot of freedom. Many women born decades ago never divorced not because they didn't want to, but because they could not afford it.

I mentioned divorce to show an extreme case, a lack of freedom so big that the whole relationship depends on it. But even on small things, lack of freedom can become tiring and wear the relationship.

But what happens if one of the partners does not work? Or do both need to have an income? I'll tell you a story, and this time it is not about imaginary friends... It's a couple I know well, born in 1942 (both of them). The husband worked most of his life (they are both retired now). But you know what? He never managed his salary. He gave it all to his wife. And then it was the wife who gave him pocket money...

I find this a very creative solution. You see, having to ask for money to the partner who holds the purse can be problematic. But if the person holding the purse is not the "breadwinner", the whole process is reversed.

I am giving this as a hint, something to consider and adapt. However, *if one of the partners has no income, the other should make him/her independent and not dependent.* The difference is huge... Giving the partner a reasonable sum on a regular basis as s/he wishes is a good solution, without then using it as a tool to make him/her feel "inferior".

Forcing one partner to ask for money every time and even worse explain why s/he needs it is humiliating to say the least.

Variety

Nothing is as tiring for a couple as "the same all over again every day, day in day out with no end in sight." Sometimes one of the partners leads the couple into a very routine life pattern. Sometimes both do it.

The fact is that routines are comfortable, and we feel safe with them. And indeed, you do need to have *some routines in your life and relationship.* The problem starts when routines are too many, and one of the partners starts feeling a bit bored.

Boredom within a relationship is frustrating, and one of the most common causes of this is actually the television... That very handy box of entertainment is not a good friend of happy relationships. I know, it is comfortable, it is cheap, and above all, it is *there.* Gong to the pictures requires the "going bit" ... It is also more expensive, it takes time, you need to get dressed... Especially if you are tired from work, the television is far too tempting.

But how many couples spend virtually every evening in front of the television? And how often do you think a couple should go out?

I usually find that when the "going out" starts becoming less than once a week, we may be entering "boredom territory". Not necessarily. I base this on the average urban couple. In the countryside dynamics may be different. You see, if you are indoors in an apartment in a city, you end up stuck in front of the television. If, however you live in the countryside, the glass of wine or cup of tea under a star-studded sky is often much more appealing than a reality show or even a sitcom... Certainly more than the news!

That can be romantic, and I would count it as "going out". But keep that general rule as guideline: ***at least once a week try to do something different, go out, have fun...***

And don't do the same thing every week. That restaurant you love so much because you went there on your first date can skip a week and you can try something different instead.

And how about when you have children? Big question. If you live near your parents or in-laws, or if you have friends that can help, do try to keep this "once a week we have fun" pattern.

If you don't? Well, babysitters are an option, if you can afford one. Maybe a friend who needs some extra cash, a student etc. Or... Why don't you do a thing like "car sharing?" Let me explain... Why don't you find friends with a child roughly as old as yours? Then you can do like this:

- On one day, you go out and they look after your child.
- On another day, they go out and you look after their child.
- On yet another day, you can meet at yours or theirs...

You get the extra bonus of a social evening, which in any case is a good break from routine evenings!

Communication

Ok, this has been the focus of most of this book. Still, it is so important that it is worth repeating... But there is a key thing you need to understand about communication:

- *It is easy to have good communication in a couple if you start off open communication early on in your relationship.*

So, if you are at the first stages of your relationship, or if you are about to start one, do not waste those first few months. *Get into the habit of talking things through amicably and openly as early as possible.* Once you have developed this habit try to keep it. Actually, do everything in your power to keep this habit alive.

Be careful, because if *there is a communication breakdown, and the couple "go silent" it is much harder to reintroduce it.* By now you must have realized that in psychology and sociology we can never underestimate *"the power of habit".* It's like smoking and all bad habits. We pick them up, often without even being conscious of them. But once something has become a habit, it is hard to break.

If you are in one of those relationships that "have gone silent" work on reintroducing communication over a long time and in small steps. Here are some tips:

- *Start with easy to face topics*. Don't start with the most emotional and problematic issue you have if it is possible.
- Have *short, friendly, but frequent chats*. One big open-hearted chat followed by months of silence will not become a pattern, a habit, a "new modus vivendi"...
- *Allow your partner to get used to it*. Be understanding and patient, people take time to change traits of their behavior.
- *Consider that your partner may feel some level of embarrassment*. There can be some discomfort with new habits and talking about intimate things after a long time can be embarrassing.
- *Always end on a positive note!* Don't leave any bitter aftertaste to your partner or s/he will find it even harder to take on this new habit you want to introduce. Instead, close with something very positive. Your partner must be able to look back on the chat and feel *comfortable about it.*
- For this reason, *have lots of chats about positive things.* We tend to talk about things only when there is a problem. Especially in relationships. But hey, find an excuse and have an open-hearted chat about something positive. A long but heartfelt compliment is perfect. "I need to tell you how proud I am that you have taken up the art class and I love your style..." This sort of conversation is perfect to restart the communication after long breaks but also to keep it alive. So, even if you are so lucky that you don't have any problem at all for months or years, find a positive excuse to keep this habit alive. It may come in very handy later on...

So, frequency, positivity, good endings, short chats, and then a bit of bonding are excellent qualities of these chats. And your relationship may well depend on them!

A Common Mission

A common mission can be a panacea for relationships. Remember when we talked about the dynamics of relationships? Some are closed onto themselves... What happens then? All stress coming from within and outside the relationship is released inside, pushed in, like when you pump a bicycle tire. This may well cause the tire to burst... actually, it is easier to make a relationship burst with pressure from outside than even a weak tire.

While if you have a common mission, you will have a valve, an outlet, or even better a channel to turn pressure from outside into something positive and constructive.

Some couples are actually formed around a common mission, objective, passion, or goal. If you met your partner through an action group or charity, then of course you will already share a passion.

But what about if you didn't? The answer is simple, try to find one as early as possible in your relationship. It can be a small, local cause like, even feeding the cats of the neighborhood, it does not need to be anything particularly serious, demanding and complex. Actually, choose something achievable. Wanting to save the world is all good but it might be asking too much of your relationship...

And this leads us to our next point.

A Sense of Complicity

Doing things together, working on a common project can keep alive that sense of complicity that great relationships have. Don't underestimate this. When you are in the role of accomplices, you are "equals collaborating towards a common goal". That greatly improves mutual understanding and even communication.

It is also a way of getting to know each other while at the same time *learning to trust each other.* And of course, trust is next.

Trusting Each Other

We all say that trust is indispensable in a relationship. And in fact, it is. Lack of trust can lead to sad situations and, above all, *unnecessary jealousy.* Losing someone's trust is also very damaging, because most people never forgive those who break their trust and never give it back. It is often a permanent choice, and a couple cannot survive unless trust is kept or, if it is lost, it is then regained.

But how can you make sure that your relationship keeps being a trustful one? There are many ways, and, of course the main is **never to do anything that can cost you your partner's trust.** Before you do something, think about the consequences.

On the other hand, sometimes trust "fades a bit" instead of dissolving completely all of a sudden like a snowflake in the Sun... There is nothing big and traumatic, like an affair behind your back, but little by little things may become "less bright".

On the whole the older a relationship gets, the more trust there is within it. But this seems to become more prominent after a few years (usually 7 – that watershed of most relationships!) Before this mark, it may sometimes wane a bit.

This can also be due to lifestyle matters. If one of the partners is often absent for work, one of the partners has a wide (working) social network, if one of the partners travels a lot, while the other does not have these things, then it may happen that the second partner may become a bit jealous and lose a bit of trust.

What can you do about it then? Oddly enough it is again down to communication. Have very regular and very *frequent open and honest conversations.* The topic can be whatever you want, from world affairs to your friends or even yourselves. But have them, short, open, no secrets... That alone can greatly improve the level of trust in a relationship and reduce episodes of jealousy.

Playfulness

Oh, yes! Keep feeling young inside, actually keep that childish playfulness alive in your relationship. We make strong bonds with our playmates, don't we? Then absolutely keep playing games. Very playful couples even invent "in games" which is games they play alone, and know how to play.

These are sometimes played at parties, with friends, and even practical jokes can be fun. But do keep in mind that when others are involved, you should always mean no harm...

Then again there are many games you can play when you are alone, and even when it comes to intimacy, a bit of harmless playfulness can be wonderful. It will help you make those famous switches, but it can also help you experiment and try out new things.

What is more, it can teach you not to take yourselves too seriously…

Fun and Laughter

Please, please, please laugh as much as you can. And do it *with your partner (not at your partner,* of course). If you like telling jokes, go ahead. If you like in jokes, build as many as you wish. But even if you are not a comedian yourself, try to share funny moments with your partner.

Here the television (or a video platform, or the old-fashioned VCR… it does not matter) may come in handy. Watch sitcoms, funny movies and stand-up shows. Indeed, make sure that you have a "laughing evening" at least once a week, and every single week. And please, do treat yourself to that stand-up comedian you love so much when s/he has a show near where you live!…

It will be a great night out with your partner, so, something great to do, but it is also a "serotonin therapy" for your relationship. And I cannot even begin to list the positive effects of serotonin (a hormone released when we laugh) on your health, mental abilities, mood, emotional life, stress level, and even on your social and personal relationships. And in fact, I won't – start that is…

Friendship

Finally, do keep that friendship side of your relationship always kindled and alive. Going out with friends helps that, but also, as we said, playing together. The important thing is that you always treasure your partner also as a friend.

In fact, in super happy relationships the partners also see each other and treat each other also as best friends. And when they are out with others, they don't so much appear as a "romantic couple" but as a "pair of beat friends". That in turn helps the wider circle of friends stay young, compact, and united.

I know, at this stage I usually tease you about the next chapter. But not this time. In fact, there is no other chapter at all... What follows next is a goodbye from me, or maybe it is au revoir?

CONCLUSION

Wow, wow, wow have we not come a long way?! Remember when we first met? I do, I remember the first steps in this book... And look at what you know now! You are now basically an expert of relationships. And I don't mean a person who's had many... I mean that you have a good understanding of what relationships are like, how they work, what they need, and how you can face them with confidence, without anxiety, and without insecurities.

Actually – let me tell you – I think now you are confident and competent enough to give some good and sound tips to your friends. Do you want to have a go? Shall we try out a final exercise just for fun (and because I have become totally addicted to tea by now...)

Think about some friends of yours who are in a relationship. Have you got any tips on how to improve it (or to straighten up some "creases" in their relationship)?

And I know you have come up with an awful lot of ideas... But this is not just to look back and see the huge progress you have made...This is also a tip for you... Yes, thinking about your friends' relationships. You don't even need to then tell them what you have come up with. That is, unless you really think they would accept it and benefit from it... No, the reason is that *it is safer to "brainstorm ideas" for other people's relationships.* It is safer for your relationship. It's just a mental exercise, while if you did it about yourself and your partner it would be "something more" already.

So, *use being an agony aunt even if only in your mind, about your friends' relationships as training, to develop your own skills, and only then apply your best ideas to your relationship!*

I bet you did not expect a final "trick of the trade" in the conclusion of this book... You would laugh to be inside a psychologist's mind on a train... They often make little "thought experiments" with the passengers. Like working out if there is an issue, what the issue may be like etc... It is just training with a skill, with a technique. And you can do the same now.

Let's try to remember a few of the many amazing things we have discovered about relationships in this book... For example, maybe you came thinking that a relationship is fixed, that it should never change? Well, now you know quite well that this very thought is what causes lots of anxiety, insecurities, and even major problems.

In fact, now you know that relationships change and go through many stages. But that there are also many different dynamic types in relationships... Some are closed and some are open, some are inclusive, others exclusive, some one directional, others not, some are egalitarian, others are not...

And you now know that the key to a happy relationship is not to be nostalgic of the first phase, the infatuation phase... that is a fairy tale idea.... But have you noticed that all fairy tales stop as soon as the relationship actually starts for real? Then they don't tell you the truth about Snow White... Dear Prince Charming turned out to be an utter bore and she went back to the Seven Dwarfs! Joking aside, that is to remind you that **to be happy within a relationship both partners need to be comfortable with it at any stage**. And this often **involves changing the relationship.** Things change and you need to change with them. You can't have the same lifestyle before and after you have a baby. Ask any mum or dad... Actually, you don't even need to ask, look at their eye bags for the first year or so and you will already guess that many things have changed, even in the bed department...

But now you also know that **communication is core to relationships and their success.** We have spent quite a lot of time learning how we can communicate effectively. Remember that there is a **specific way to express emotions, even when you are having an important talk...** But you also know that communication needs to be kept alive. Many, frequent, positive and honest chats are what keep relationships alive and happy.

Those relationships where the partners keep things to themselves for weeks, months – even years – then all comes out in a massive row that lasts for a full day and that people in the near town confuse for fireworks... Those relationships have serious problems. But those where the partners talk frequently in most cases never even get to that stage where the massive argument starts.

But in case, you now know the way *professionals avoid, defuse, and de-escalate arguments,* and you can apply it to your relationship. Or even explain it to your friends if you have some who argue far too much. They will thank you for it.

But again, you now know that there are many types, or archetypes as we called them, of relationships and *being confident with your relationship also means finding the right recipe, the right balance of traits from all these archetypes.*

And again, we have seen how *important it is to be able to switch smoothly in a relationship.* It is in fact a technique that has been developed oddly enough by a very unexpected community, remember? But psychology is not judgmental, and we take lessons wherever we can get one.

Many other things have made this journey what it has been. I hope you found it useful informative, colorful, and sometimes even fun, because laughing helps remembering things! And I hope you liked all my "imaginary friends". On this topic, just an ethical point: psychologists have to hide the identity of their patients when they talk about them, even in formal academic studies, the names are all fake, but the stories are real...

And I certainly have enjoyed it, and I hope you have too.

And if you need me again, you know where you can find me... No – not in the cupboard; that's where I drink my addictive teas... you can find me on a shelf!

RESOURCES

And if you want to know more, if you want to develop an area we have seen in this book a bit more in detail, here are some very useful books for you to choose from!

April, P. C. (2020). *The Anxiety Getaway: How to Outsmart Your Brain's False Fear Messages and Claim Your Calm Using CBT Techniques (Science-Based Approach to Anxiety Disorders)*. Mango.

Bancroft, L. (2003). *Why Does He Do That?: Inside the Minds of Angry and Controlling Men* (Reprint ed.). Berkley Books.

Berne, E. (2016). *Games People Play: The Psychology of Human Relationships* (Penguin Life) (01 ed.). Penguin Life.

Butler, G. (2021). *Overcoming Social Anxiety and Shyness, 2nd Edition: A self-help guide using cognitive behavioural techniques* (Overcoming Books) (2nd ed.). Robinson.

Deguchi, H. (2021). *THE REAL RICH LIFE: Unlock the Secrets of Relationships.* Independently published.

Douglas, G. M. (2013). *Divorceless Relationships.* Access Consciousness Publishing Company.

Evans, P. (2010). *The Verbally Abusive Relationship, Expanded Third Edition: How to recognize it and how to respond* (Third ed.). Adams Media.

Hill, C., & Sharp, S. (2020). *How to Stop Overthinking: The 7-Step Plan to Control and Eliminate Negative Thoughts, Declutter Your Mind and Start Thinking Positively in 5 Minutes or Less.* Indy Pub.

Kingma, D. R. (1998b). *A Lifetime of Love: How to Bring More Depth, Meaning and Intimacy Into Your Relationship (Lasting Love, Deeper Intimacy, & Soul Connection)* (2nd ed.). Conari Press.

Life, T. S. O., & Botton, D. A. (2018). *Relationships (The School of Life Library)* (Illustrated ed.). The School of Life.

Ma, C. A. (2017). *The Anxiety Workbook: A 7-Week Plan to Overcome Anxiety, Stop Worrying, and End Panic* (Workbook ed.). Althea Press.

MacKenzie, J., & Thomas, S. (2019). *Whole Again: Healing Your Heart and Rediscovering Your True Self After Toxic Relationships and Emotional Abuse.* Tarcher Perigee.

Odessky, H., & Duffy, J. (2017). *Stop Anxiety from Stopping You: The Breakthrough Program For Conquering Panic and Social Anxiety.* Mango Media.

Welwood, J. (2007). *Perfect Love, Imperfect Relationships: Healing the Wound of the Heart* (42095th ed.). Trumpeter.

Winston, D. (2017). *The Smart Girl's Guide to Polyamory: Everything You Need to Know About Open Relationships, Non-Monogamy, and Alternative Love.* Skyhorse.

CPSIA information can be obtained
at www.ICGtesting.com
Printed in the USA
LVHW110204260422
717225LV00005B/303